day
skipper
Updated 2011

Written by Penny Haire
Illustrations by Sarah Selman
Edited by Sara Hopkinson
and Simon Jinks

www.rya.org.uk

Royal Yachting Association
RYA House, Ensign Way, Hamble, Southampton SO31 4YA
Tel: 0844 556 9555 Fax: 0844 556 9516
email: training@rya.org.uk website: www.rya.org.uk

CONTENTS

The skills required to skipper a boat safely, navigate from port to port and moor up at the end of the day are the same the world over. However, there are two notable differences that can catch-out the unwary sailor when sailing in different parts of the world; the circulation of weather patterns in the Northern and Southern Hemispheres and the layout of buoyage in the Eastern and Western Hemispheres. Both of these differences are covered in the book, but ensure you use the correct system for your sailing area.

Charts reproduced throughout this book are for training purposes only. On no account should they be used for navigation.

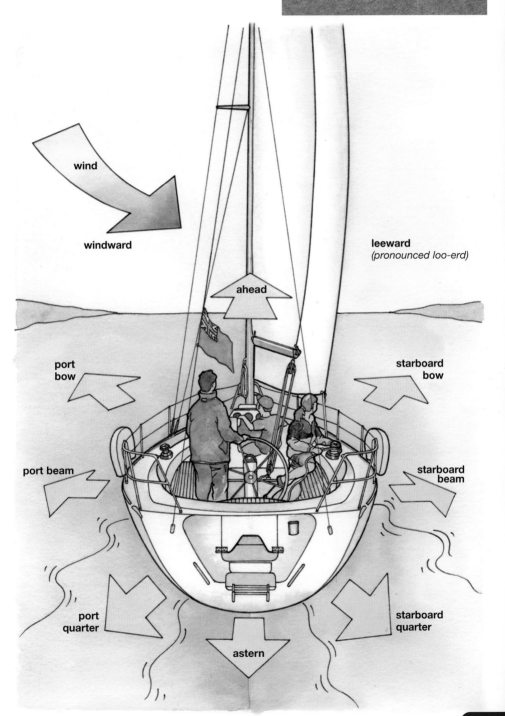

wind

windward

leeward
(pronounced loo-erd)

ahead

port
bow

starboard
bow

port beam

starboard
beam

port
quarter

starboard
quarter

astern

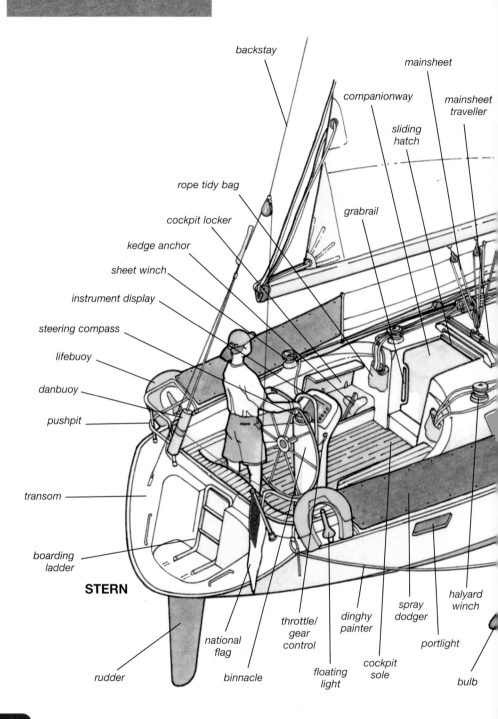

backstay

mainsheet

companionway

mainsheet traveller

sliding hatch

rope tidy bag

grabrail

cockpit locker

kedge anchor

sheet winch

instrument display

steering compass

lifebuoy

danbuoy

pushpit

transom

boarding ladder

STERN

halyard winch

spray dodger

throttle/ gear control

dinghy painter

national flag

portlight

rudder

binnacle

floating light

cockpit sole

bulb

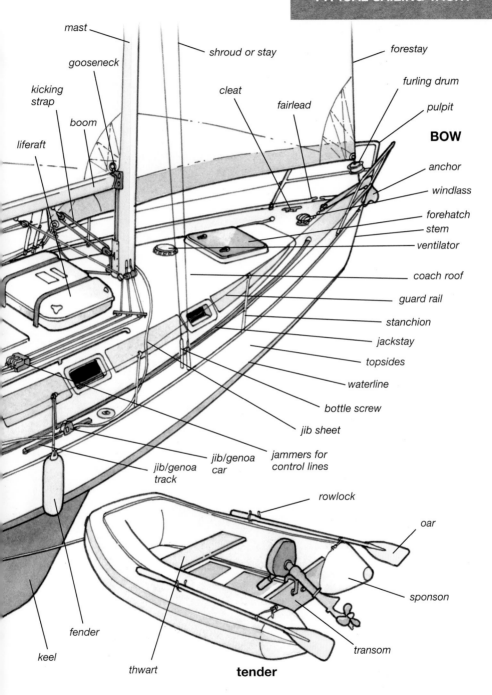

mast

shroud or stay

forestay

gooseneck

furling drum

kicking strap

cleat

pulpit

boom

fairlead

BOW

liferaft

anchor

windlass

forehatch

stem

ventilator

coach roof

guard rail

stanchion

jackstay

topsides

waterline

bottle screw

jib sheet

jammers for control lines

jib/genoa car

jib/genoa track

rowlock

oar

sponson

fender

transom

keel

thwart

tender

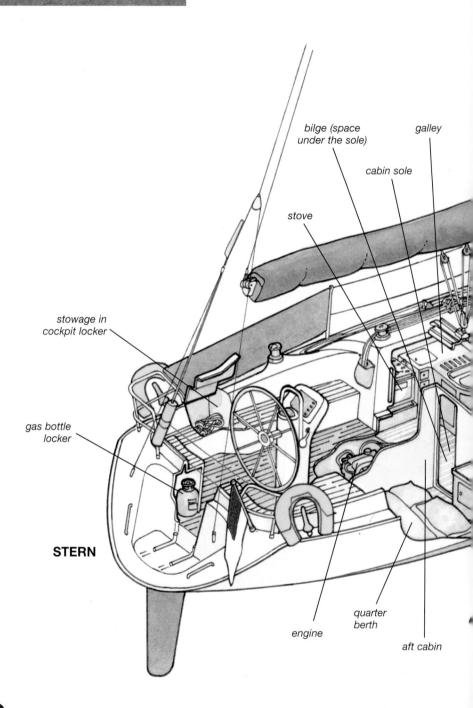

bilge (space under the sole)

galley

cabin sole

stove

stowage in cockpit locker

gas bottle locker

STERN

engine

quarter berth

aft cabin

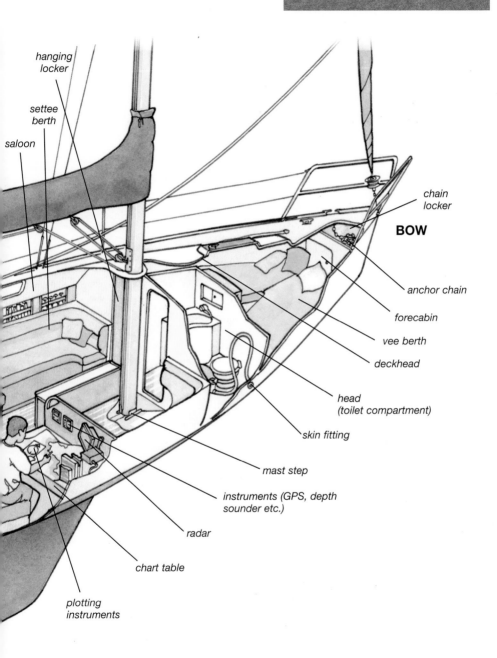

hanging locker

settee berth

saloon

chain locker

BOW

anchor chain

forecabin

vee berth

deckhead

head (toilet compartment)

skin fitting

mast step

instruments (GPS, depth sounder etc.)

radar

chart table

plotting instruments

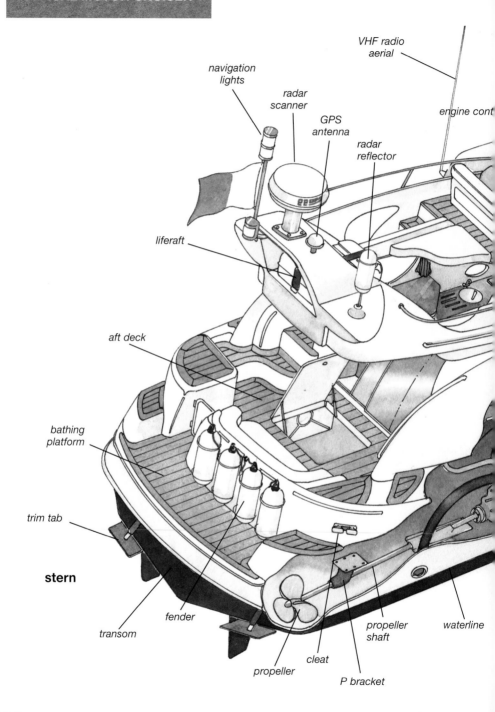

VHF radio
aerial

navigation
lights

radar
scanner

GPS
antenna

engine cont

radar
reflector

liferaft

aft deck

bathing
platform

trim tab

stern

transom

fender

propeller

cleat

propeller
shaft

P bracket

waterline

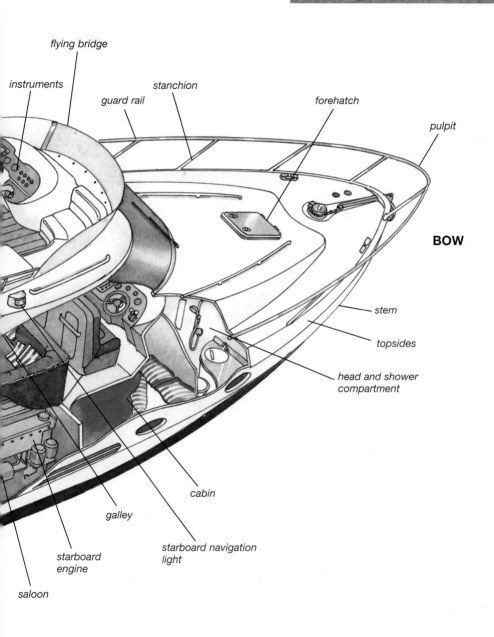

flying bridge

instruments

stanchion

guard rail

forehatch

pulpit

BOW

stem

topsides

head and shower
compartment

cabin

galley

starboard navigation
light

starboard
engine

saloon

You can't sail closer than about 45° to the wind otherwise the sails flap and the boat slows down very quickly

To make progress to windward (into the wind) you must travel in a series of zigzags, each at 45° to the wind.

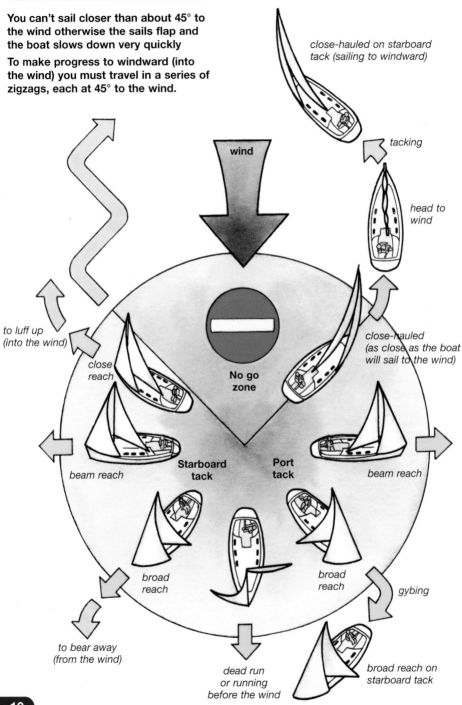

close-hauled on starboard tack (sailing to windward)

wind

tacking

head to wind

close-hauled (as close as the boat will sail to the wind)

to luff up (into the wind)

close reach

No go zone

Starboard tack

Port tack

beam reach

beam reach

broad reach

broad reach

gybing

to bear away (from the wind)

dead run or running before the wind

broad reach on starboard tack

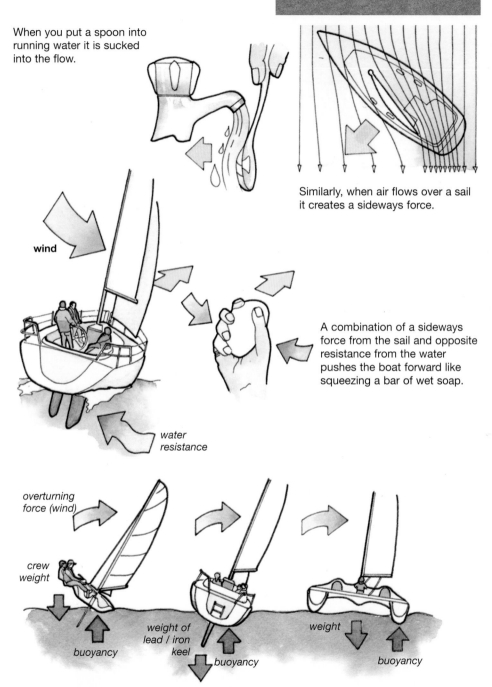

When you put a spoon into running water it is sucked into the flow.

Similarly, when air flows over a sail it creates a sideways force.

wind

A combination of a sideways force from the sail and opposite resistance from the water pushes the boat forward like squeezing a bar of wet soap.

water resistance

overturning force (wind)

crew weight

buoyancy

weight of lead / iron keel

buoyancy

weight

buoyancy

A sailing boat does not blow over as the force of the wind is counterbalanced by weight and buoyancy.

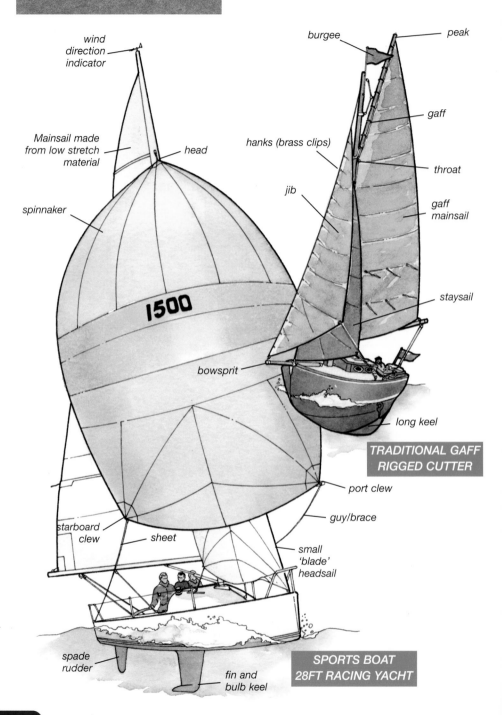

wind direction indicator

burgee

peak

gaff

Mainsail made from low stretch material

head

hanks (brass clips)

throat

spinnaker

jib

gaff mainsail

1500

staysail

bowsprit

long keel

TRADITIONAL GAFF RIGGED CUTTER

port clew

guy/brace

starboard clew

sheet

small 'blade' headsail

spade rudder

fin and bulb keel

SPORTS BOAT 28FT RACING YACHT

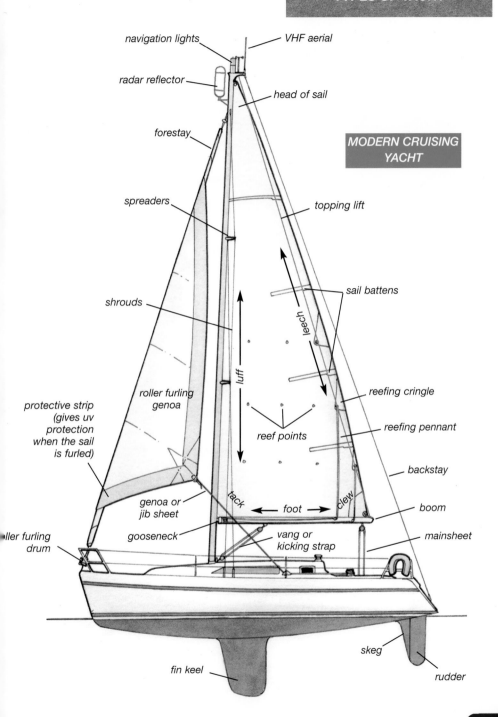

navigation lights

VHF aerial

radar reflector

head of sail

forestay

**MODERN CRUISING
YACHT**

spreaders

topping lift

sail battens

shrouds

leech

luff

roller furling
genoa

reefing cringle

protective strip
(gives uv
protection
when the sail
is furled)

reef points

reefing pennant

backstay

genoa or
jib sheet

tack

foot

clew

boom

roller furling
drum

gooseneck

vang or
kicking strap

mainsheet

skeg

fin keel

rudder

13

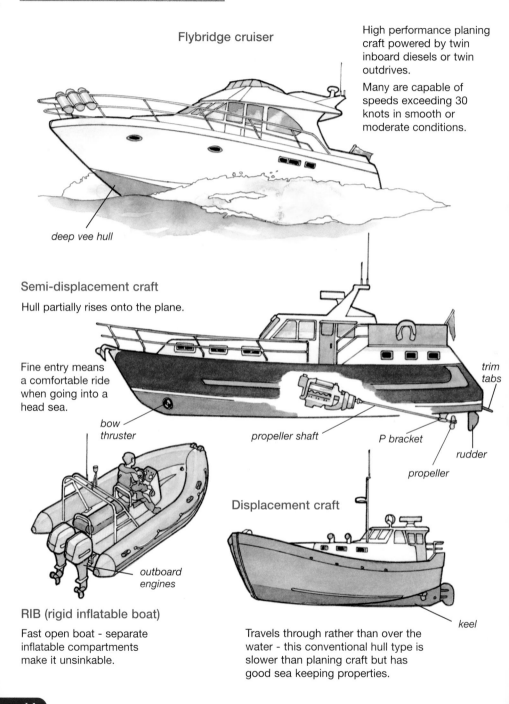

Flybridge cruiser

High performance planing craft powered by twin inboard diesels or twin outdrives.

Many are capable of speeds exceeding 30 knots in smooth or moderate conditions.

deep vee hull

Semi-displacement craft

Hull partially rises onto the plane.

Fine entry means a comfortable ride when going into a head sea.

bow thruster

propeller shaft

P bracket

trim tabs

rudder

propeller

Displacement craft

outboard engines

RIB (rigid inflatable boat)

Fast open boat - separate inflatable compartments make it unsinkable.

Travels through rather than over the water - this conventional hull type is slower than planing craft but has good sea keeping properties.

keel

High performance planing craft

boat rides over the surface of the water

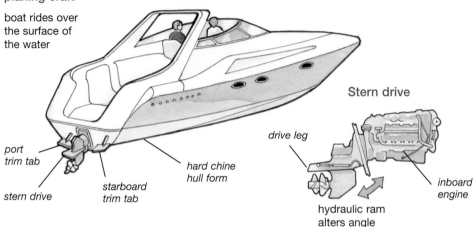

port trim tab

stern drive

starboard trim tab

hard chine hull form

Stern drive

drive leg

inboard engine

hydraulic ram alters angle

TRIM

Changing the trim will affect the way a boat behaves in different conditions. Experiment to find how your boat reacts.

Power trim

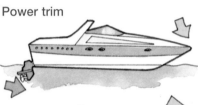

Outdrive leg in - drops the bow for going into a head sea reduces slamming

Outdrive leg out - lifts the bow in a following sea

Trim tabs in operation

Both tabs down = Bow down

Port tab = Port up

Both tabs up = Bow up

Starboard tab = Starboard up

Rolling hitch

Used when you need a knot that won't slip when pulled at an angle. Ideal for taking the strain off another rope.

Round turn and two half hitches

Multipurpose knot. Can be untied under tension.

Reef knot

Mainly used for tying in reef points. Not very secure.

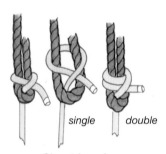

single   *double*

Sheet bend

Used for joining two ropes.

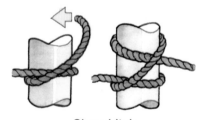

Clove hitch

Quick to tie and easy to adjust. Ideal for securing fenders.

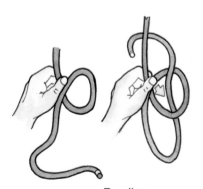

Bowline

Makes a fixed eye in a rope which is very secure but can't be untied under tension. Many uses such as attaching jibsheets to sails and for loops in mooring lines.

Figure of eight

Easy to tie stopper knot - stops rope escaping.

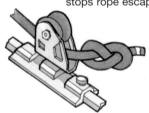

Making fast to a cleat

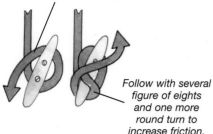

Rope led to 'open' side of cleat.

Follow with several figure of eights and one more round turn to increase friction.

Jammer - holds rope securely, like a cleat.

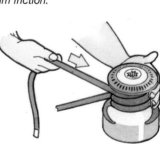

when releasing a rope under load don't hold it close to the jammer - take the strain on a winch.

Winching techniques

Using a winch gives more power for pulling in ropes

Use the selftailer to grip the rope before you winch

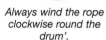

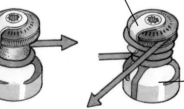

Add more turns for maximum friction.

Always wind the rope clockwise round the drum'.

Turn the handle either way to pull in the rope.

Keep the lead low to avoid a riding turn.

When letting out gently ease rope round drum with palm of hand.

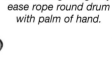

 Always have your thumbs uppermost - take care not to trap fingers or thumbs between the rope and the winch

 Never wrap the rope around your hand.

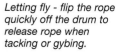

Letting fly - flip the rope quickly off the drum to release rope when tacking or gybing.

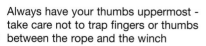

ALONGSIDE A WALL

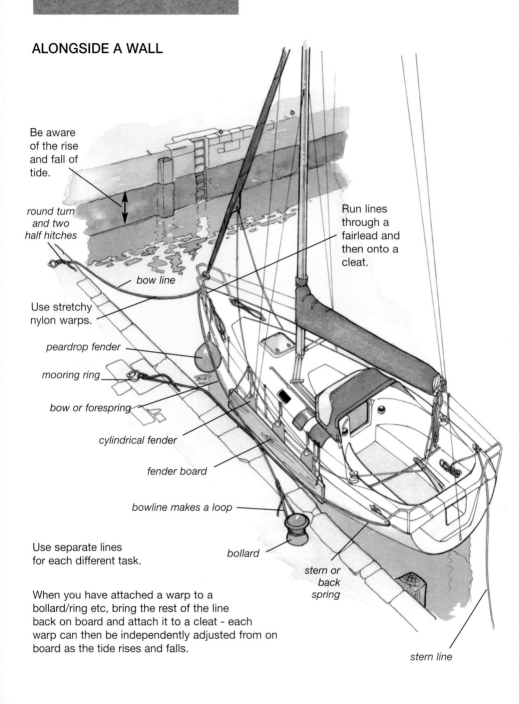

Be aware of the rise and fall of tide.

round turn and two half hitches

Run lines through a fairlead and then onto a cleat.

bow line

Use stretchy nylon warps.

peardrop fender

mooring ring

bow or forespring

cylindrical fender

fender board

bowline makes a loop

bollard

stern or back spring

Use separate lines for each different task.

When you have attached a warp to a bollard/ring etc, bring the rest of the line back on board and attach it to a cleat - each warp can then be independently adjusted from on board as the tide rises and falls.

stern line

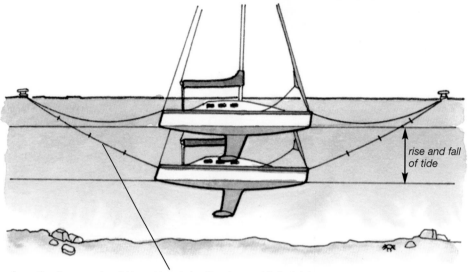

Length of warps should be at least 4 x the rise and fall of tide.

rise and fall of tide

In a raft

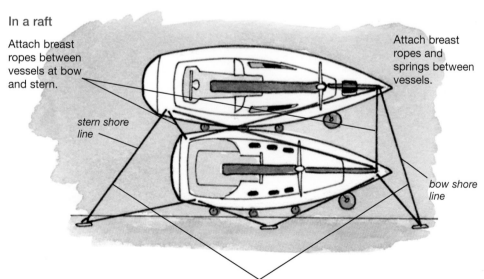

Attach breast ropes between vessels at bow and stern.

Attach breast ropes and springs between vessels.

stern shore line

bow shore line

Outside boat should take bow and stern lines ashore to minimise strain on the inside boat's shore lines.

ON A FLOATING PONTOON

You should not have to
adjust lines as the tide
rises and falls.

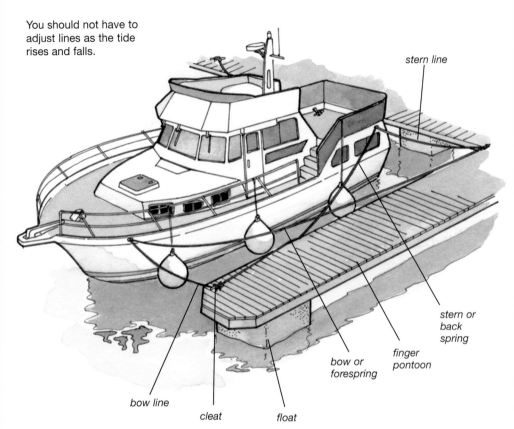

stern line

*stern or
back
spring*

*finger
pontoon*

*bow or
forespring*

bow line

cleat

float

IN A PEN

Stern lines are attached to piles and the bow lines are attached to a wall or pontoon. Usually the windward lines are attached first.

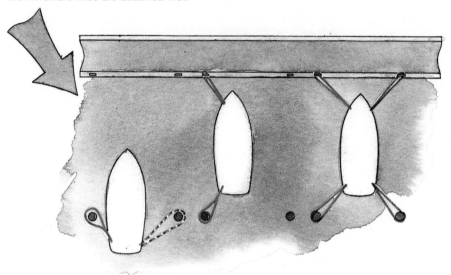

In some countries one of the piles is replaced by a pontoon for ease of access to the shore. The lines are ajusted to allow access from the steps or amidships. Pick-up-lines are usually supplied on the piles to aid retrieval.

bow line

ring rises and falls with tide

pick-up lines

stern line

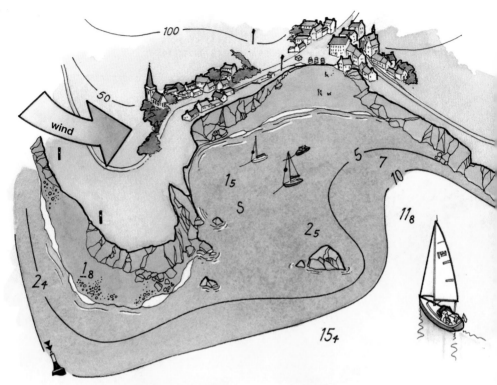

Selecting an anchorage

- Will you be sheltered? - look for maximum protection from wind, swell and tide. Check forecast for possible changes of wind direction.

- What is the sea bed like? - look at the chart symbols - mud and sand give better holding than rock or shingle.

- What will the tide do during your stay? - calculate the tide times and heights - make sure that you don't pick a spot where you will go aground as the tide falls.

- Will you have enough swinging room? - allow for other boats, isolated rocks etc.

- Prepare the amount of anchor chain or warp that you need before dropping the anchor.

You don't necessarily need to anchor at the position of the anchor symbol. This is just a recommendation.

Avoid anchoring on or near the leading line - other boats may be coming in.

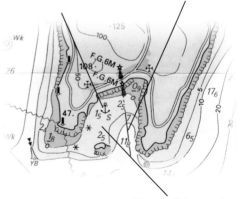

There will be much less tidal flow in the bay than outside.

Scope

The scope of chain or warp you need depends on the maximum depth of water you expect during your stay.

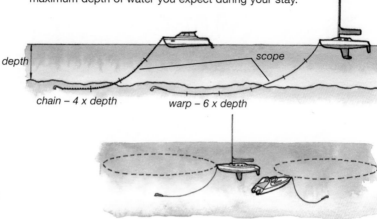

chain – 4 x depth   warp – 6 x depth

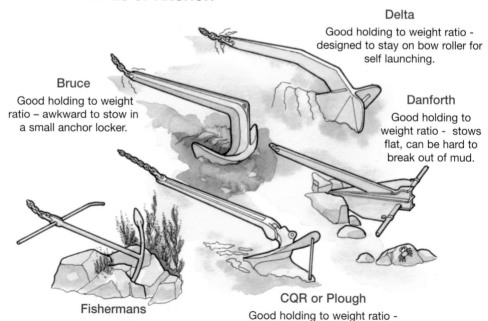

Always allow enough swinging room to account for wind and tide. Bear in mind that light/flat-bottomed boats will lie differently to deeper draft/low windage boats.

TYPES OF ANCHOR

Delta
Good holding to weight ratio - designed to stay on bow roller for self launching.

Bruce
Good holding to weight ratio – awkward to stow in a small anchor locker.

Danforth
Good holding to weight ratio - stows flat, can be hard to break out of mud.

Fishermans
Traditional type, good for rocky & weedy bottoms – awkward to stow and poor holding power in sand and mud.

CQR or Plough
Good holding to weight ratio - hard to stow and moving parts can capsize.

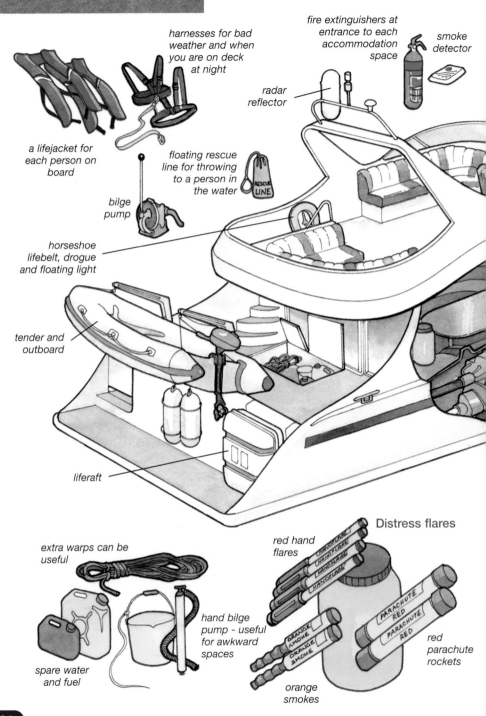

harnesses for bad weather and when you are on deck at night

fire extinguishers at entrance to each accommodation space

smoke detector

radar reflector

a lifejacket for each person on board

floating rescue line for throwing to a person in the water

RESCUE LINE

bilge pump

horseshoe lifebelt, drogue and floating light

tender and outboard

liferaft

extra warps can be useful

spare water and fuel

hand bilge pump - useful for awkward spaces

Distress flares

red hand flares

HANDFLARE
HANDFLARE
HANDFLARE
HANDFLARE

ORANGE SMOKE
ORANGE SMOKE

orange smokes

PARACHUTE RED
PARACHUTE RED

red parachute rockets

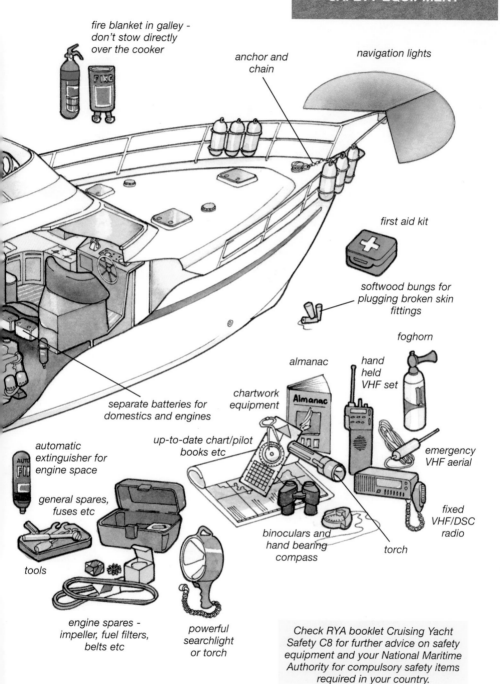

fire blanket in galley - don't stow directly over the cooker

anchor and chain

navigation lights

first aid kit

softwood bungs for plugging broken skin fittings

foghorn

almanac

hand held VHF set

chartwork equipment

Almanac

separate batteries for domestics and engines

emergency VHF aerial

automatic extinguisher for engine space

up-to-date chart/pilot books etc

fixed VHF/DSC radio

general spares, fuses etc

binoculars and hand bearing compass

torch

tools

engine spares - impeller, fuel filters, belts etc

powerful searchlight or torch

Check RYA booklet Cruising Yacht Safety C8 for further advice on safety equipment and your National Maritime Authority for compulsory safety items required in your country.

Clothing

Man-made fibres layered to trap air for warmth. Avoid wearing cotton clothing underneath waterproofs.

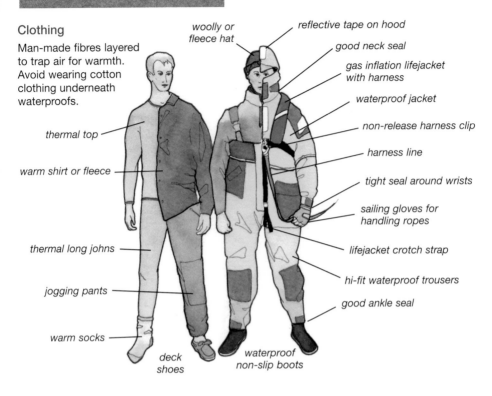

woolly or fleece hat

reflective tape on hood

good neck seal

gas inflation lifejacket with harness

waterproof jacket

non-release harness clip

harness line

tight seal around wrists

sailing gloves for handling ropes

lifejacket crotch strap

hi-fit waterproof trousers

good ankle seal

thermal top

warm shirt or fleece

thermal long johns

jogging pants

warm socks

deck shoes

waterproof non-slip boots

Seasickness & hypothermia

Stay warm & dry

Eat and drink regularly

Take seasickness remedies

Symptoms of seasickness

Lethargic/disinterested - pale colour

Symptoms of hypothermia

Shivering, pale colour, irrational behaviour, disoriented

Ultra violet rays are harmful, may cause skin cancer and impair vision.

Reflection from the water increases the effect of the sun.

Wear a wide brimmed hat and/or one with neck protection. Use sun glasses with 100% UV protection.

Regularly apply sun block of SPF 30 – 40.

Wear loose long sleeved shirts and trousers.

Try to avoid exposure between 11am - 3pm – take a long lunch and seek shade. Biminis and cockpit tents are ideal shelters.

Babies and toddlers are especially susceptible to UV damage – keep them out of the sun or well protected.

Wear shoes to protect feet from hot decks and stubbing toes

Dehydration is caused by vomiting, sweating and simply not drinking enough fluids. It can lead to shock and hyperthermia – heatstroke.

Dehydration Symptoms

Mild - thirst, dry lips, dark urine colour. Remedy: Rehydrate using water and/or with an oral re-hydrating solution

Moderate – partial heatstroke. Very dry mouth, sunken eyes, skin looses elasticity. Remedy: Rehydrate casualty under close supervision and seek medical guidance.

Severe – heatstroke. All of above plus rapid, weak pulse, rapid breathing, confused, lethargic. Remedy: Get medical help quickly and re-hydrate.

 DON'T EXCEED THE ALCOHOL LIMIT.

Common causes of fire

 Smoking below decks

 Solvents/paints stored below

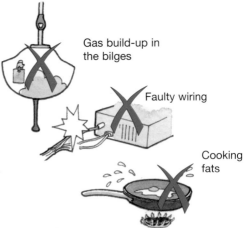

Gas build-up in the bilges

Faulty wiring

Cooking fats

Extinguishers

Dry powder – don't use on flammable liquids
CO_2/Halocarbon – good for enclosed spaces
AFFF - foam, good for flammable liquids

Blanket – good for smothering flames and if clothing is on fire

Petrol/Gasoline vapour

Always vent engine space before starting an inboard petrol engine.

Keep outboards on deck to avoid the build-up of petrol vapour below.

Gas safety

Butane and propane can be highly dangerous.

To clear gas - open hatches and turn downwind to vent fresh air through the boat

Bilge pumps are designed to pump water - many won't clear gas very effectively

Keep gas bottle in a sealed locker that drains overboard

Shut-off valve inside near cooker

Escaping gas is heavier than air and will sink into bilges

Don't attempt DIY repairs to your system - always call in a qualified fitter.

Location of extinguishers

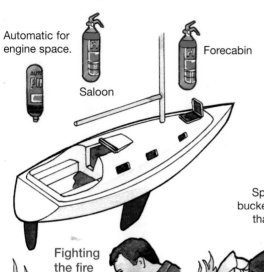

Automatic for engine space.

Saloon

Forecabin

Extinguishers should be to hand near the exit to each accommodation space.

The engine space should have its own dedicated extinguisher which is automatic or can be activated remotely without having to open the engine compartment and let in oxygen.

Splashing water from a bucket can be more effective than throwing its entire contents at once.

Fighting the fire

Aim the extinguisher at the base of the flames.

Fire blankets can be used to smother a galley fire.

Protect your hands when using a fire blanket.

They are also essential for clothing fires.

REMEMBER

The boat will fill up with smoke very quickly.

- Get everyone on deck with a lifejacket.
- You may have to send a Mayday/fire distress flares etc.

If you cannot fight the fire
BE PREPARED TO ABANDON SHIP

Boating is generally a safe pastime but, should the worst happen, make sure you and your crew know what to do.

Use a pinpoint flare (night) or an orange smoke (day).

Put on a lifejacket.

Alert the coastguard.

ABANDONING TO THE LIFERAFT

Make sure the painter is tied on.

Board raft from the yacht. Stay dry.

Throw raft to leeward and tug painter to inflate.

Put heaviest, strongest crew in first to stabilise the raft and assist others in boarding.

Once aboard
- cut painter
- paddle away
- stream drogue
- close door
- take seasickness tablets
- keep as warm and dry as possible
- ventilate interior every hour

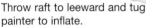

RESCUE

- The lifeboat coxswain will need to talk to you to assess the situation.
- Make sure there are no lines in the water which could foul the lifeboat's propeller.

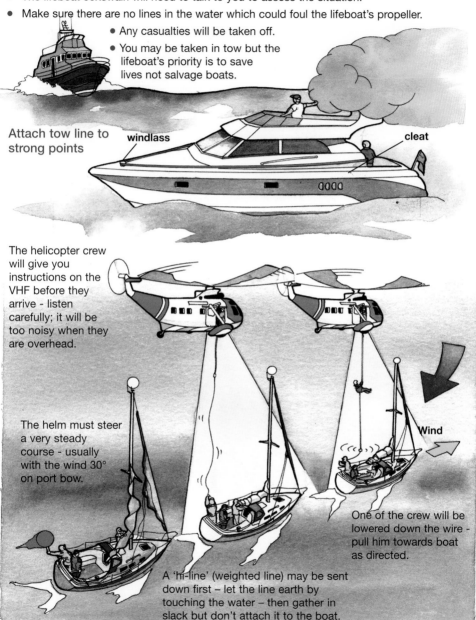

- Any casualties will be taken off.
- You may be taken in tow but the lifeboat's priority is to save lives not salvage boats.

Attach tow line to strong points

windlass

cleat

The helicopter crew will give you instructions on the VHF before they arrive - listen carefully; it will be too noisy when they are overhead.

The helm must steer a very steady course - usually with the wind 30° on port bow.

Wind

One of the crew will be lowered down the wire - pull him towards boat as directed.

A 'hi-line' (weighted line) may be sent down first – let the line earth by touching the water – then gather in slack but don't attach it to the boat.

Methods may vary depending on the country and organisation, some lower rescue cages, and some recommend reefing, not lowering the mainsail.

VHF VOICE CALL

Use VHF to alert the coastguard and other vessels in your area.

You must tell them:

- your boat's name
- your position
- how many people are on board
- what assistance you require.

VHF is better than a mobile phone for distress calling - other vessels in your area will hear your call and the coastguard can use VHF transmissions to fix your position.

A mobile phone will only tell one person that you are in trouble; the network coverage is patchy away from land and you won't be able to talk direct to a helicopter or lifeboat.

DIGITAL VHF (DSC) CALL

You may not have time to send a voice call but some modern VHF sets can:

- send a distress alert or urgency call at the press of a button
- be linked to a GPS to give your position.

045°(T) from Colville Point 3.2M

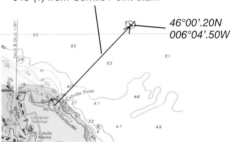

46°00'.20N
006°04'.50W

MAYDAY	PAN PAN
When life or vessel are in grave and imminent danger	**Urgency message - if crew or vessel need assistance**
Mayday x 3	Pan Pan x 3
This is motor yacht *Puffin* x 3	All ships x 3
Mayday yacht *Puffin*	This is yacht *Seaspray* x 3
(give MMSI if Distress Alert sent)	(give MMSI if Urgency Alert sent)
In position 46°00'.20N 006°04'.50W	In position 045°(T) from Colville Point Lighthouse 3.2M
Holed and sinking	I have a broken rudder and require a tow
Require immediate assistance	Four persons on board
Six persons on board	Over
Over	

You may use a VHF radio under the supervision of a qualified person or to make a distress call - otherwise you need an operator's certificate. Contact the RYA or your National Maritime Authority for details of courses.

FLARES

NEVER fire a parachute rocket if a helicopter is approaching.

Fire rocket vertically.

If windy fire 15° downwind.

In low cloud fire at 45°.

Handheld pinpoint flare shows exactly where you are - use inshore or in sight of other vessels.

wind

NEVER fire into the wind.

Orange smoke for use by day - especially in bright sunlight.

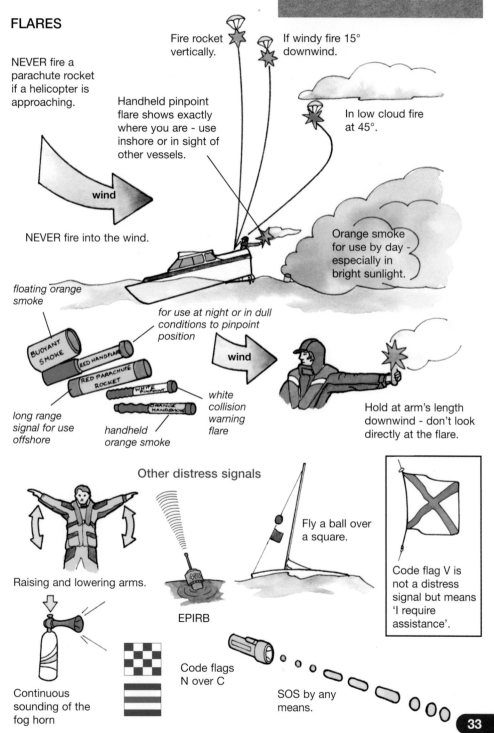

floating orange smoke

for use at night or in dull conditions to pinpoint position

wind

BUOYANT SMOKE

RED HANDFLARE

RED PARACHUTE ROCKET

WHITE PINPOINT

ORANGE HANDSMOKE

white collision warning flare

long range signal for use offshore

handheld orange smoke

Hold at arm's length downwind - don't look directly at the flare.

Other distress signals

Raising and lowering arms.

EPIRB

Fly a ball over a square.

Code flag V is not a distress signal but means 'I require assistance'.

Continuous sounding of the fog horn

Code flags N over C

SOS by any means.

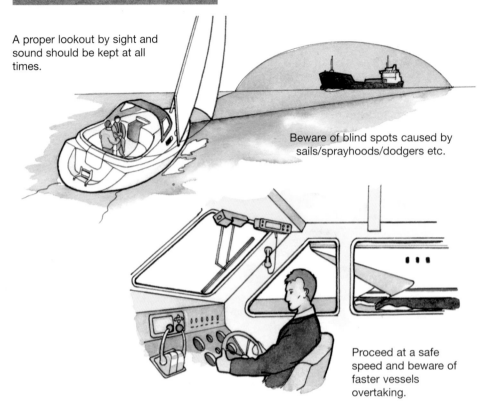

A proper lookout by sight and sound should be kept at all times.

Beware of blind spots caused by sails/sprayhoods/dodgers etc.

Proceed at a safe speed and beware of faster vessels overtaking.

How can we tell if a risk of collision exists?

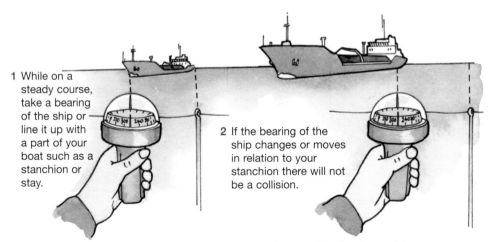

1 While on a steady course, take a bearing of the ship or line it up with a part of your boat such as a stanchion or stay.

2 If the bearing of the ship changes or moves in relation to your stanchion there will not be a collision.

If the bearing stays steady or the ship remains lined up with your stanchion - a risk of collision exists.

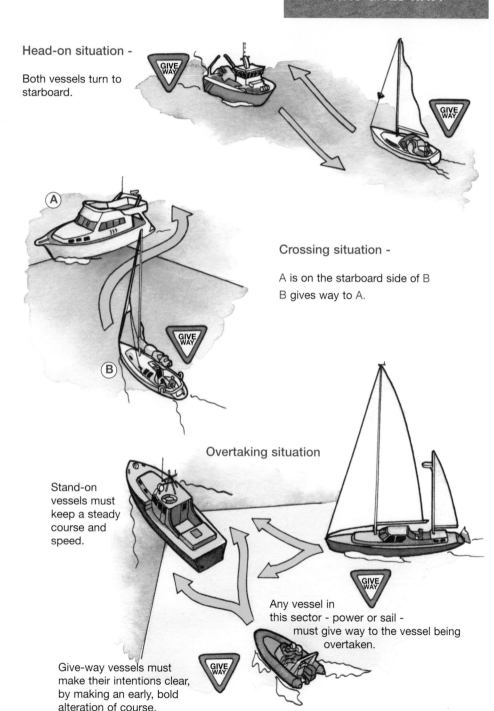

Head-on situation -

Both vessels turn to starboard.

Crossing situation -

A is on the starboard side of B
B gives way to A.

Overtaking situation

Stand-on vessels must keep a steady course and speed.

Any vessel in this sector - power or sail - must give way to the vessel being overtaken.

Give-way vessels must make their intentions clear, by making an early, bold alteration of course.

GIVE WAY

35

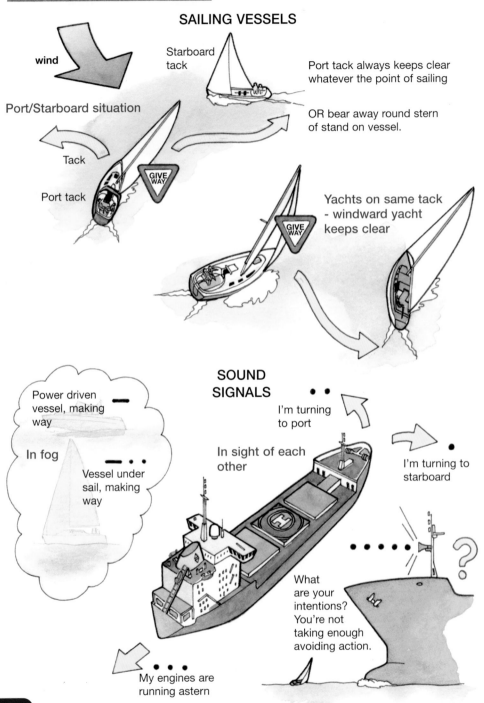

SAILING VESSELS

wind

Starboard tack

Port tack always keeps clear whatever the point of sailing

Port/Starboard situation

OR bear away round stern of stand on vessel.

Tack

GIVE WAY

Port tack

Yachts on same tack - windward yacht keeps clear

GIVE WAY

SOUND SIGNALS

Power driven vessel, making way —

In fog

Vessel under sail, making way — . .

In sight of each other

I'm turning to port • •

I'm turning to starboard •

What are your intentions? You're not taking enough avoiding action. • • • • •

My engines are running astern • • •

NARROW CHANNELS

Power does not necessarily give way to sail when both are navigating in a narrow channel.

Large vessels rely on keeping up their speed to be able to manoeuvre - don't impede them.

If you need to cross a channel your heading should be at 90° to channel.

In most cases small craft can sail outside the main channel – check the chart.

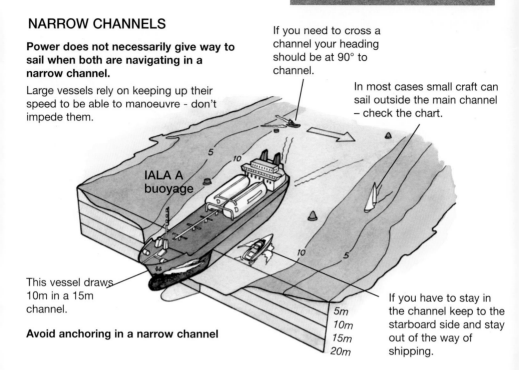

IALA A buoyage

This vessel draws 10m in a 15m channel.

Avoid anchoring in a narrow channel

5m
10m
15m
20m

If you have to stay in the channel keep to the starboard side and stay out of the way of shipping.

IN ORDER OF PRIORITY

The International Regulations for the Prevention of Collision at Sea (IRPCS) is mostly common sense - a more manoeuvrable vessel must not impede the less manoeuvrable one.

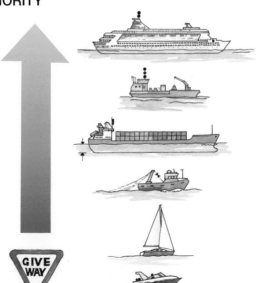

Not under command

Restricted in ability to manoeuvre

Constrained by draught

Fishing

Sailing

Power driven vessel

GIVE WAY

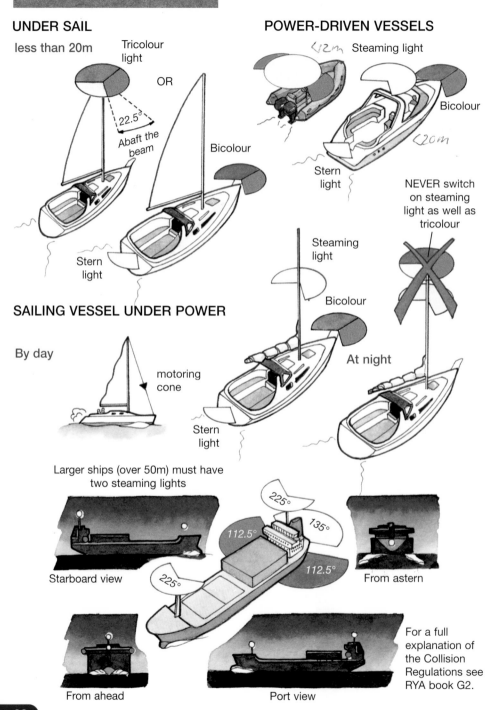

UNDER SAIL

less than 20m

Tricolour light

OR

22.5°

Abaft the beam

Bicolour

Stern light

Stern light

POWER-DRIVEN VESSELS

<2m   Steaming light

Bicolour

<20m

Stern light

NEVER switch on steaming light as well as tricolour

SAILING VESSEL UNDER POWER

By day

motoring cone

Steaming light

Bicolour

At night

Stern light

Larger ships (over 50m) must have two steaming lights

Starboard view

225°

112.5°

135°

112.5°

From astern

225°

From ahead

Port view

For a full explanation of the Collision Regulations see RYA book G2.

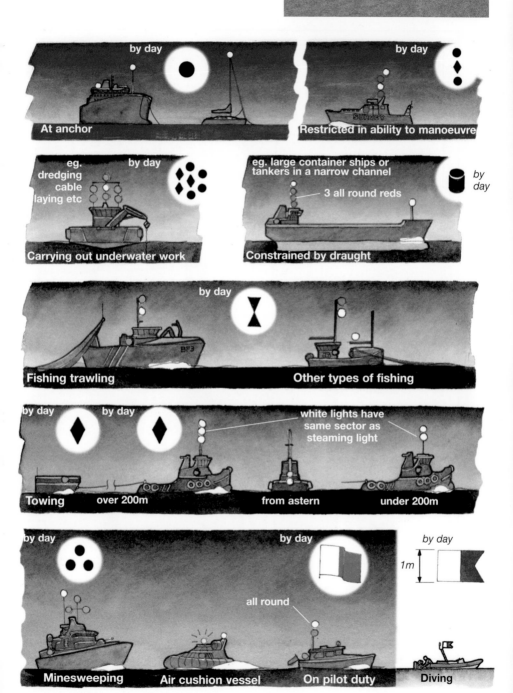

At anchor — by day

Restricted in ability to manoeuvre — by day

Carrying out underwater work — eg. dredging cable laying etc — by day

Constrained by draught — eg. large container ships or tankers in a narrow channel — 3 all round reds — by day

Fishing trawling — by day — **Other types of fishing**

Towing — by day — by day — over 200m — white lights have same sector as steaming light — from astern — under 200m

Minesweeping — by day — **Air cushion vessel** — all round — **On pilot duty** — by day — by day — 1m — **Diving**

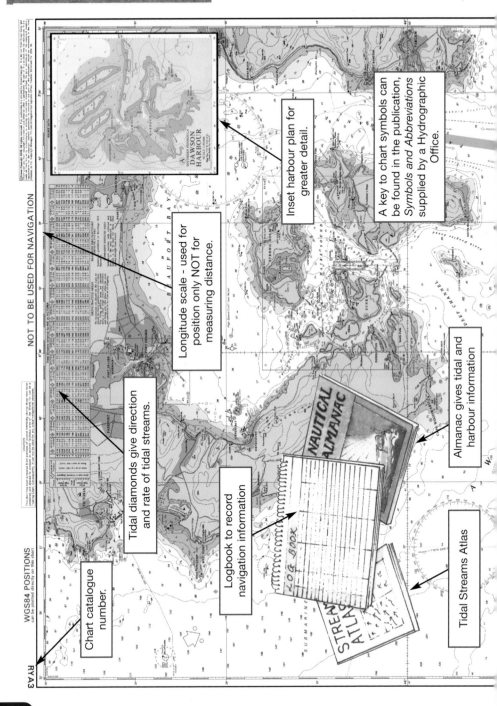

NOT TO BE USED FOR NAVIGATION

WGS84 POSITIONS
can be plotted directly on this chart

RYA3

Inset harbour plan for greater detail.

A key to chart symbols can be found in the publication, *Symbols and Abbreviations* supplied by a Hydrographic Office.

Longitude scale – used for position only NOT for measuring distance.

Tidal diamonds give direction and rate of tidal streams.

Almanac gives tidal and harbour information

Logbook to record navigation information

Chart catalogue number.

Tidal Streams Atlas

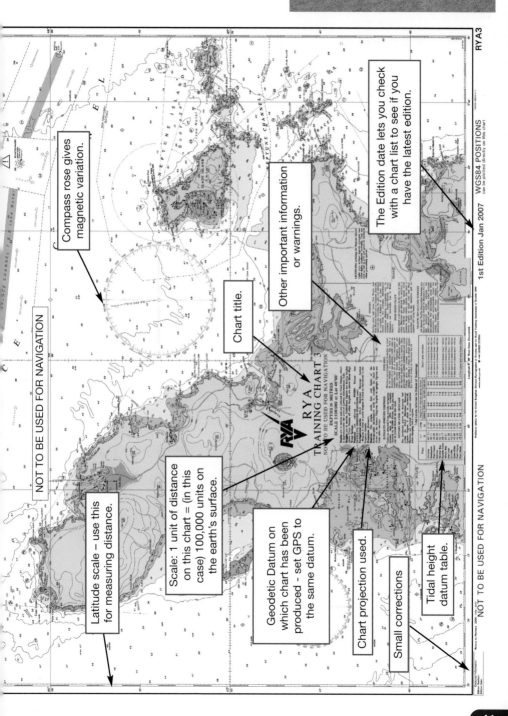

Compass rose gives magnetic variation.

The Edition date lets you check with a chart list to see if you have the latest edition.

Other important information or warnings.

Chart title.

Scale: 1 unit of distance on this chart = (in this case) 100,000 units on the earth's surface.

Latitude scale – use this for measuring distance.

Geodetic Datum on which chart has been produced - set GPS to the same datum.

Chart projection used.

Small corrections

Tidal height datum table.

NOT TO BE USED FOR NAVIGATION

NOT TO BE USED FOR NAVIGATION

RYA
TRAINING CHART 3
NOT TO BE USED FOR NAVIGATION

1st Edition Jan 2007

WGS84 POSITIONS
can be plotted directly on this chart

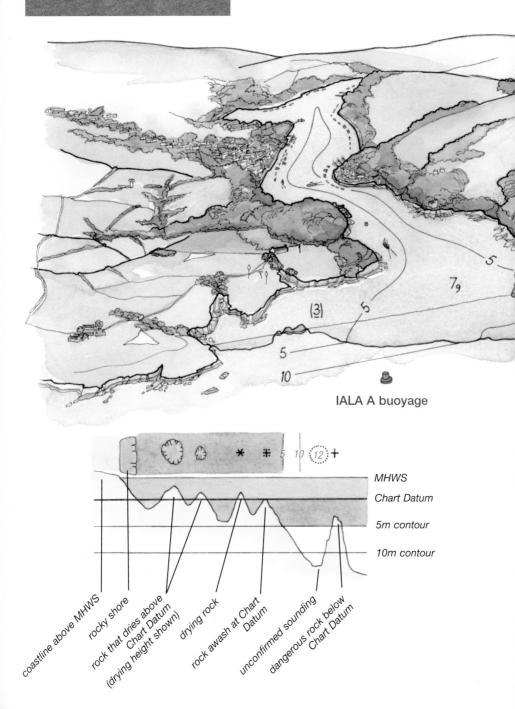

IALA A buoyage

MHWS

Chart Datum

5m contour

10m contour

coastline above MHWS

rocky shore

rock that dries above Chart Datum (drying height shown)

drying rock

rock awash at Chart Datum

unconfirmed sounding

dangerous rock below Chart Datum

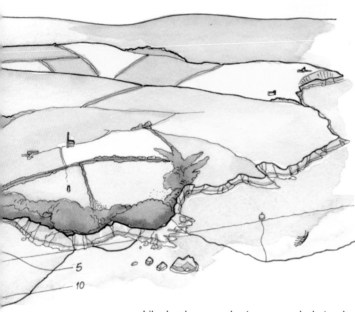

Like land maps, charts use symbols to show useful and important features. Information is carefully chosen to show hazards clearly and to help identify features that are visible from a boat at sea.

Symbols & Abbreviations published by a Hydrographic Office can be used to identify features and symbols on the chart.

⊥   *Beacon*

⊕   *Yacht harbour/marina*

⌂   *Can buoy*

╫   *Wreck, depth unknown, not considered dangerous to surface navigation*

⊞   *Battery, small fort*

ʄ   *Chimney*

▨   *Steep coast, cliffs*

◣   *Building*

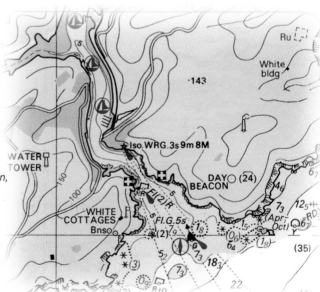

IALA A buoyage

BY LATITUDE AND LONGITUDE

Lines of Longitude run from pole to pole dividing the earth into segments rather like an orange.

Lines of Latitude are obtained by projecting angles made from the centre of the earth to points on its surface.

Distance and speed

For all practical purposes a mile at sea is 1852 metres.

1° = 60' minutes of Latitude
1' = 1 nautical mile

Speed is measured in knots.
A knot is one nautical mile per hour.

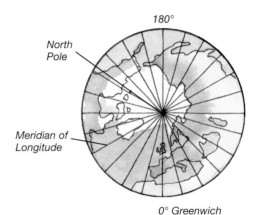

180°

North Pole

Meridian of Longitude

0° Greenwich Meridian

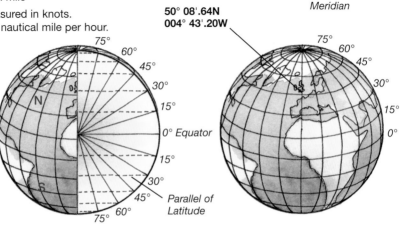

50° 08'.64N
004° 43'.20W

75°
60°
45°
30°
15°
0° Equator
15°
30°
45° — Parallel of Latitude
60°
75°

75°
60°
45°
30°
15°
0°

Plotting your position

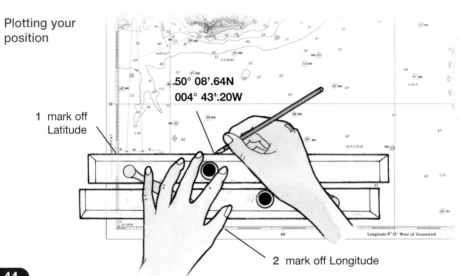

50° 08'.64N
004° 43'.20W

1 mark off Latitude

2 mark off Longitude

Longitude 4° 35' West of Greenwich

BY RANGE AND BEARING   eg. 246°(T) from South Head Lighthouse 1.6M

With a plotter

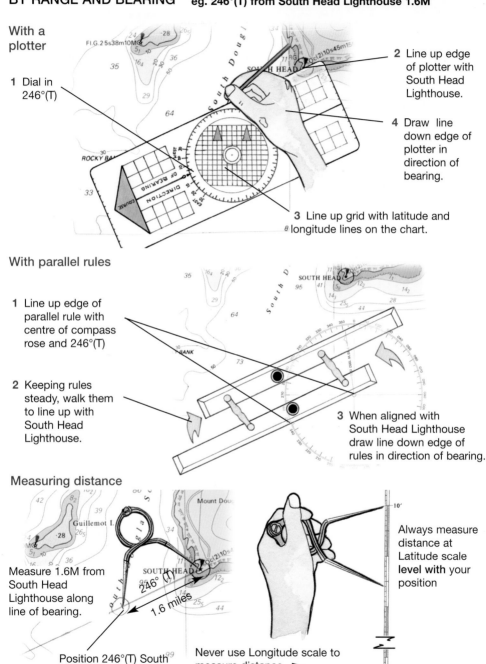

1 Dial in 246°(T)

2 Line up edge of plotter with South Head Lighthouse.

4 Draw line down edge of plotter in direction of bearing.

3 Line up grid with latitude and longitude lines on the chart.

With parallel rules

1 Line up edge of parallel rule with centre of compass rose and 246°(T)

2 Keeping rules steady, walk them to line up with South Head Lighthouse.

3 When aligned with South Head Lighthouse draw line down edge of rules in direction of bearing.

Measuring distance

Measure 1.6M from South Head Lighthouse along line of bearing.

246° (T)

1.6 miles

Position 246°(T) South Head Lighthouse 1.6M

Always measure distance at Latitude scale **level with** your position

Never use Longitude scale to measure distance.

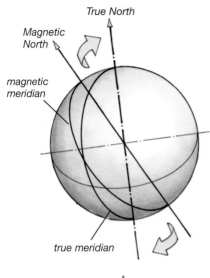

True North

Magnetic North

magnetic meridian

equator

true meridian

Charts show North as True (geographic) North. A compass can only point to Magnetic North, which changes with time and according to your position.

The difference between True and Magnetic North is called variation.

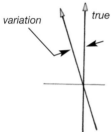

variation   true

Variation for your position is found on the nearest compass rose

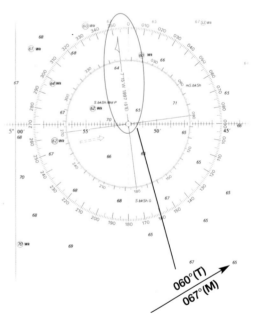

060° (T)
067° (M)

If variation is **West,** magnetic bearing is **greater** than true bearing.

If variation is **East,** magnetic bearing is **smaller.**

for example

With 5°W variation
070°(T) = 075°(M)

With 5°E variation
070°(T) = 065°(M)

Deviation is caused by ferrous metals
and electro-magnetic fields on board
which will affect the accuracy of the
compass.

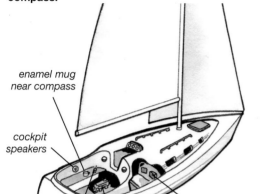

*enamel mug
near compass*

*cockpit
speakers*

mobile phone

engine

electronics

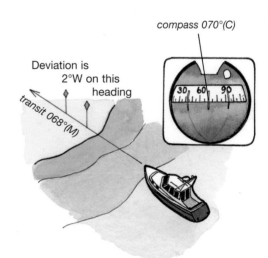

SHIPS HEAD°(C)	DEVIATION
000°	4° W
022½	2° W
045	0°
067½	2° E
090	4° E
112½	5° E
135	6° E
157½	5° E
180	4° E
202½	2° E
225	0°
247½	2° W
270	4° W
292½	5° W
315	6° W
337½	5° W
360	4° W

The ship's compass is swung to
check the effect of magnetic
influences on board, this will vary as
the boat's heading changes.

A card can be produced for your
steering compass showing the
deviation for each heading.

How to apply variation and deviation

Chartwork is in °True -
compass courses must be in °Compass

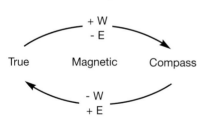

+ W
- E

True   Magnetic   Compass

- W
+ E

Finding a compass course

True bearing from chart	060°(T)
Variation	+ 7°W
Magnetic bearing	= 067°(M)
Apply deviation from card	− 2°E
Compass course	**= 065°(C)**

compass 070°(C)

Deviation is
2°W on this
heading

transit 068°(M)

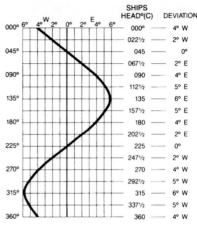

Checking for deviation

Point the boat straight at a
transit and compare results.

The gravitational pull of the moon and sun is the main cause of tides.

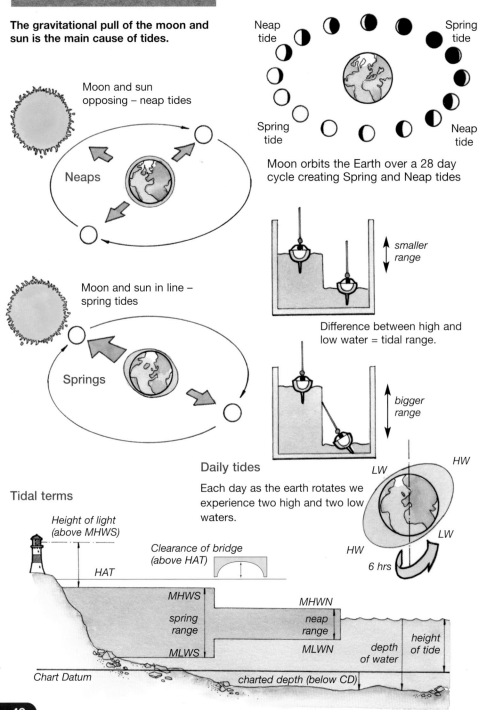

Neap tide

Spring tide

Spring tide

Neap tide

Moon and sun opposing – neap tides

Neaps

Moon orbits the Earth over a 28 day cycle creating Spring and Neap tides

Moon and sun in line – spring tides

Springs

smaller range

Difference between high and low water = tidal range.

bigger range

Daily tides

Tidal terms

Each day as the earth rotates we experience two high and two low waters.

LW   HW

HW   LW

6 hrs

Height of light (above MHWS)

Clearance of bridge (above HAT)

HAT

MHWS

spring range

MLWS

MHWN

neap range

MLWN

depth of water

height of tide

Chart Datum

charted depth (below CD)

The depth of water under your boat is measured with an echo sounder – ultrasonic signals are transmitted to and reflected from the seabed to give the depth of water on a digital or analogue display.

The transducer is sited below the waterline - allow for this when reading the display.

You can also calibrate for the display to read from waterline or bottom of keel.

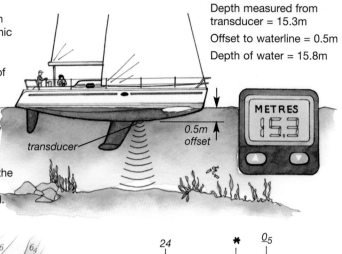

Depth measured from transducer = 15.3m

Offset to waterline = 0.5m

Depth of water = 15.8m

transducer

0.5m offset

METRES
15.3

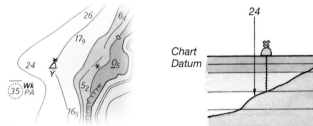

Chart Datum

24

*

0₅

5m
10m
20m
30m

Chart shows depths you are likely to meet at the lowest predicted tide – Chart Datum (CD).

16	Time	m
	0043	4.5
	0715	2.0
TU	1316	4.6
	1957	1.8
17	0206	4.7
	0835	1.7
W	1440	4.8

Height of tide is measured <u>above</u> CD

Tide tables give the times and heights of high and low water for different ports.

ADD depths below CD to the height of tide.

SUBTRACT drying heights from the height of tide.

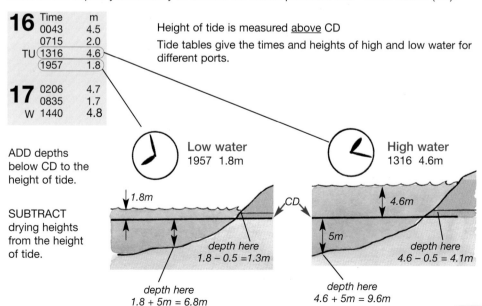

Low water
1957 1.8m

High water
1316 4.6m

1.8m

CD

4.6m

5m

depth here
1.8 – 0.5 =1.3m

depth here
4.6 – 0.5 = 4.1m

depth here
1.8 + 5m = 6.8m

depth here
4.6 + 5m = 9.6m

Standard ports – tide tables are produced for larger ports and give times and heights of high and low water for every day of the year. Tide times may need correcting for local changes, such as; differences in time zone from Universal Time (UT) and in countries operating Daylight Saving Time in summer time (BST in UK).

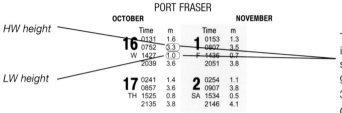

PORT FRASER

HW height

OCTOBER

	Time	m
16	0131	1.6
	0752	3.3
W	1427	1.0
	2039	3.6

LW height

	Time	m
17	0241	1.4
	0857	3.6
TH	1525	0.8
	2135	3.8

NOVEMBER

	Time	m
1	0153	1.3
	0807	3.5
F	1436	0.7
	2051	3.8

	Time	m
2	0254	1.1
	0907	3.8
SA	1534	0.5
	2146	4.1

To find out if a certain day is on springs or neaps subtract LW from HW to give the range.

3.3m - 1.0m = 2.3m

Compare this with the mean range box on the tidal curve.

Add one hour in the non shaded areas for DST.

Tidal curves

PORT FRASER 2.9m 3.3m

Use these for finding out depth of water at any time between high and low water.

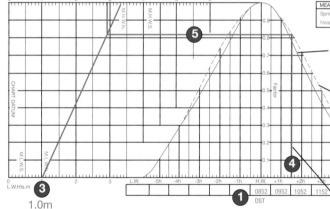

MEAN RANGES

Springs	3.8m
Neaps	2.3m

For springs use solid line (red).

For neaps use dotted line (blue).

OCTOBER

	Time	m
16	0131	1.6
	0752	3.3
W	1427	1.0
	2039	3.6

1.0m

(1020 approx)

e.g. What will be the height of tide at Port Fraser at 1020 on Wednesday 16th October?

1 enter HW (local time) and fill in the boxes for each hour after HW

2 & **3** mark in the heights of HW and LW and draw a line between them

4 find 1020 on bottom scale

5 draw line upwards to hit the curve, across to meet the HW/LW line then up to the HW scale. (Use neaps curve. HW - LW = 2.3m = neaps)

6 there will be **2.9m at 1020**

You can also find out when there will be a specific depth - i.e. at what time after HW will there be 2.0m height of tide?

Go down to the HW/LW line from the HW scale, across to the curve and down to the time scale = 1210

Secondary ports – tide tables are not produced for minor ports. To find the height and times of HW and LW at these secondary ports you will need to apply corrections, usually found in an almanac, to the times and heights of a standard port nearby.

Standard Port PORT FRASER (←)

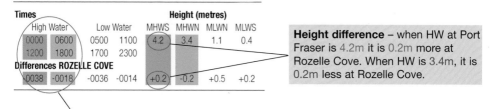

Times				Height (metres)			
High Water		Low Water		MHWS	MHWN	MLWN	MLWS
0000	0600	0500	1100	4.2	3.4	1.1	0.4
1200	1800	1700	2300				
Differences ROZELLE COVE							
-0038	-0018	-0036	-0014	+0.2	-0.2	+0.5	+0.2

Height difference – when HW at Port Fraser is 4.2m it is 0.2m more at Rozelle Cove. When HW is 3.4m, it is 0.2m less at Rozelle Cove.

Time difference – if HW Port Fraser is at 0000 or 1200 HW Roselle Cove is 38 minutes earlier but when HW Port Fraser is at 0600 or 1800 HW Roselle Cove is 18 minutes earlier.

However if HW and LW times fall between these set times you will need to interpolate between the corrections -

e.g. if HW Port Fraser is 0752 UT what time is HW at Rozelle Cove?

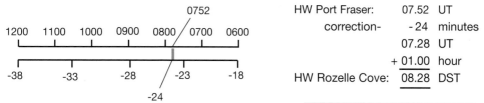

	0752	
1200 1100 1000 0900 0800 / 0700 0600		
-38 -33 -28 / -23 -18		
-24		

HW Port Fraser:	07.52	UT
correction-	- 24	minutes
	07.28	UT
	+ 01.00	hour
HW Rozelle Cove:	08.28	DST

Use the same method to interpolate height differences.

Add one hour for DST <u>after</u> calculating correction.

To find the height of tide between HW and LW at a secondary port use the tidal curve for the standard port and the secondary port data.

Use the related standard port.

For example for Rozelle Cove you should use the curve for Port Fraser.

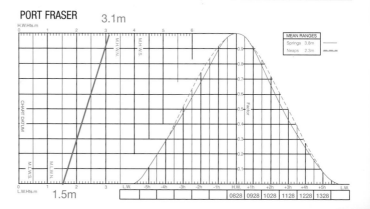

PORT FRASER   3.1m

1.5m

| | | | | | | | 0828 | 0928 | 1028 | 1128 | 1228 | 1328 | |

MEAN RANGES
Springs 3.8m
Neaps   2.3m

Consider the tide as a travelator

Go against the flow
– travel slowly

Go with the flow
– travel quickly

If you travel across the tidal
stream the boat will be
pushed sideways giving a
different ground track to the
course you are steering.

Heading

Ground track
or COG

tidal
stream

The direction and rate of tidal
streams depends on;

• your location

• whether it is springs, neaps or
between the two

• the time relative to high
water at a reference port.

FINDING THE DIRECTION AND RATE OF THE TIDE

Tidal stream atlas

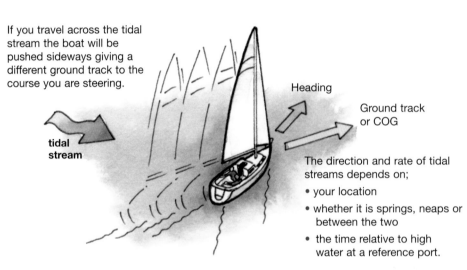

spring rate
12 = 1.2kn

neap rate
07 = 0.7kn

direction
(measure with
plotter)

time

HW Victoria

Tidal diamond from chart

Victoria Ⓑ

Hours			Ⓑ 46°20'6 N 6 18·4W		
Before High Water	6	-6	158	1·0	0·6
	5	-5	153	1·7	0·8
	4	-4	159	2·8	1·5
	3	-3	154	3·9	2·0
	2	-2	165	3·2	1·7
	1	-1	173	2·4	1·3
High Water	Ⓞ		186	1·2	0·7
After High Water	1	+1	349	1·1	0·6
	2	+2	341	3·0	1·6
	3	+3	338	3·7	1·8
	4	+4	342	3·9	2·0
	5	+5	341	2·8	1·5
	6	+6	355	2·3	1·2

spring
rate (kn)

neap
rate (kn)

direction
(°T)

time

Example

What is the direction and rate of the tidal stream 5 miles south of Namley Harbour on Friday 24th May from 1045 to 1145?

1 Find the time of HW and the heights of HW & LW at **Victoria** on Friday 24th May.

	Time	m
24	0203	1.1
	0816	5.5
F	1434	0.6
	2049	5.4

0816 UT

0916 DST is the nearest HW (say 0915)

2 Is it springs, neaps or in between?

5.5
- 0.6
range   4.9m   = Springs

MEAN RANGES		
Springs	4.9m	———
Neaps	2.4m	- - -

3 How many hours before or after HW is 1045 to 1145?

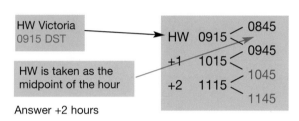

HW Victoria
0915 DST

HW is taken as the midpoint of the hour

Answer +2 hours

HW   0915 ⟨ 0845 / 0945
+1   1015 ⟨ 0945 / 1045
+2   1115 ⟨ 1045 / 1145

4 Find the nearest ◇ to your position = Ⓐ

Spring rate   = 1.6kn
Direction of tidal stream = 111°(T)

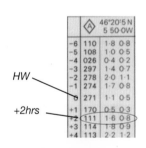

◇	46°20'5 N 5 50·0W		
-6	110	1·8	0·8
-5	108	1·0	0·5
-4	026	0·4	0·2
-3	297	1·4	0·7
-2	278	2·0	1·1
-1	274	1·7	0·8
0	271	1·1	0·5
+1	170	0·5	0·3
+2	111	1·6	0·8
+3	114	1·8	0·9
+4	113	2·2	1·2

HW
+2hrs

5 Or using a tidal stream atlas, which is the nearest arrow?

Measure direction of arrow 111°(T)

Spring rate 1.6kn

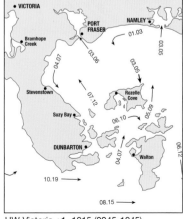

HW Victoria +1 1015 (0945-1045)

HW Victoria +2 1115 (1045-1145)

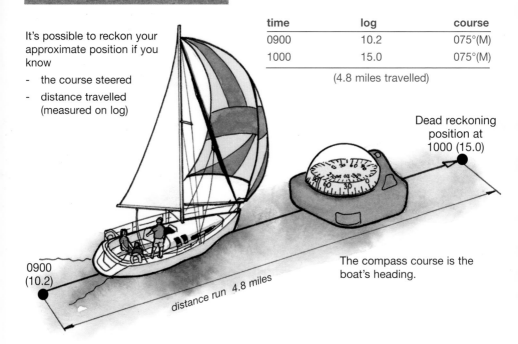

It's possible to reckon your approximate position if you know

- the course steered
- distance travelled (measured on log)

time	log	course
0900	10.2	075°(M)
1000	15.0	075°(M)

(4.8 miles travelled)

Dead reckoning position at 1000 (15.0)

0900 (10.2)

distance run 4.8 miles

The compass course is the boat's heading.

The effect of wind and tidal stream means we don't always travel in the same direction as the compass course steered.

Effect of leeway

Effect of tidal stream

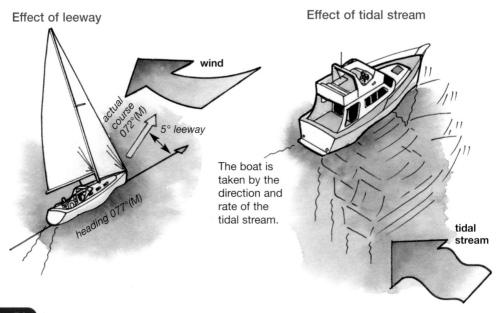

wind

actual course 072°(M)

5° leeway

heading 077°(M)

The boat is taken by the direction and rate of the tidal stream.

tidal stream

To plot an EP

time	log	course	leeway	wind	tidal stream
0900	10.2	075°(M)	0°	N5	
1000	15.0	075°(M)	0°	N5	120°(T) 2.0kn for 0900-1000

Course steered	075° (M)
Variation	- 7°W
Water track	= 068° (T)

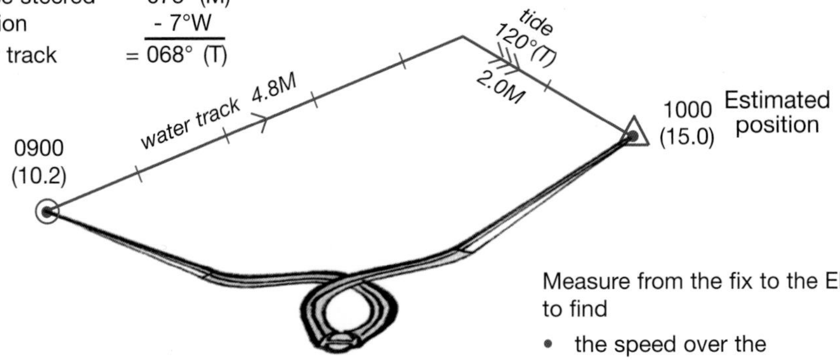

tide
120°(T)
2.0M
water track 4.8M
0900
(10.2)
1000
(15.0)
Estimated
position

Measure from the fix to the EP to find

- the speed over the ground (SOG)
- and use the plotter to find what the course over the ground (COG) has been

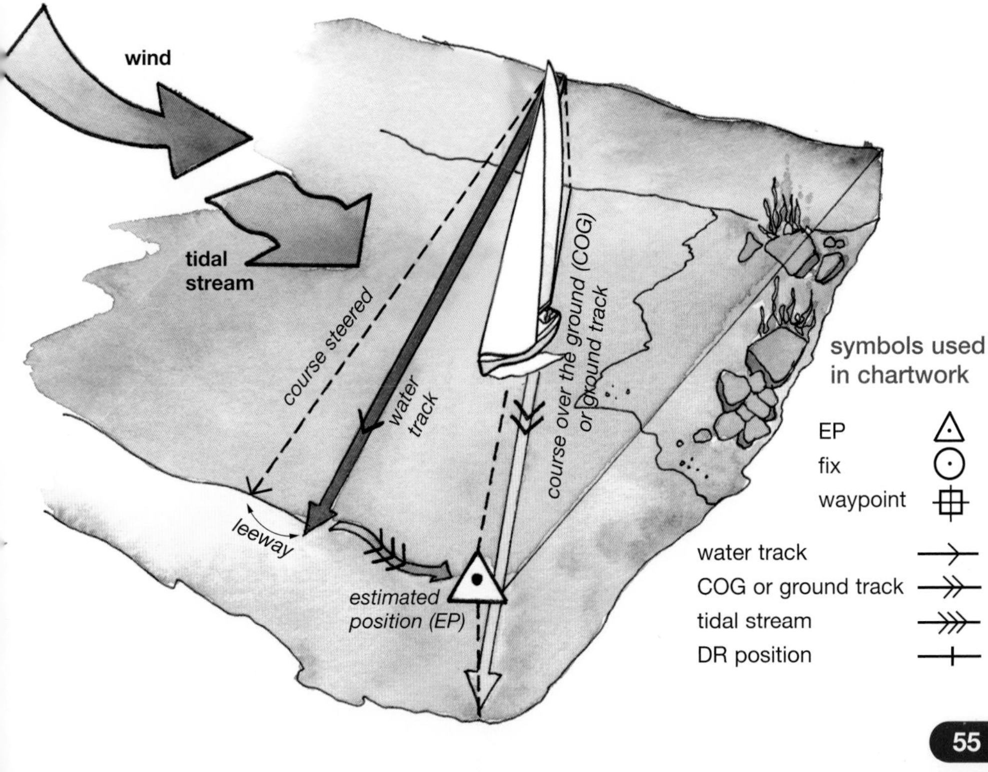

wind
tidal
stream
course steered
water
track
leeway
course over the ground (COG)
or ground track
estimated
position (EP)
symbols used
in chartwork
EP
fix
waypoint
water track
COG or ground track
tidal stream
DR position

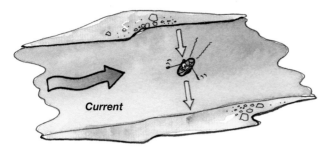

A person rowing across a river instinctively angles the boat upstream to counter the effect of the current.

At sea we often can't see our destination so we need to calculate how much to angle into the tidal stream to make the most direct passage.

Current

For example:

What is the course to steer from position A to WPT B at 1045 DST on Friday 24th May?

1 How far is it from A to B?

Answer - 8¹/₂ miles

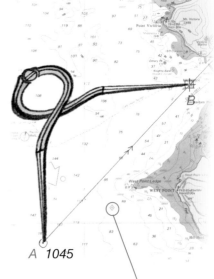

2 Approximately how long will it take to travel 8¹/₂ miles if my speed is 9 knots?

Answer – roughly an hour.

3 Leaving position A at 1045 how will the tidal stream affect my passage for the next hour?

i) Using RYA Chart 3 find the tidal stream reference port (Victoria).

ii) Find the time of HW and establish springs or neaps.

Friday 24th HW Victoria = 0916 DST range 4.9 (springs).

iii) Use the closest diamond, tidal diamond, ⟨B⟩ to establish rate and direction (you could also use a tidal atlas).

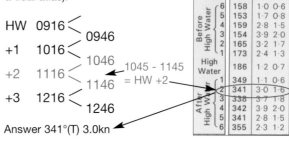

HW   0916
         0946
+1   1016
         1046   1045 - 1145
+2   1116   = HW +2
         1146
+3   1216
         1246

Answer 341°(T) 3.0kn

Hours		ⓐ 46°20'6 N	ⓑ 6 18·4W
Before High Water	6	158	1·0 0·6
	5	153	1·7 0·8
	4	159	2·8 1·5
	3	154	3·9 2·0
	2	165	3·2 1·7
	1	173	2·4 1·3
High Water		186	1·2 0·7
After High Water	1	349	1·1 0·6
	2	341	3·0 1·6
	3	338	3·7 1·8
	4	342	3·9 2·0
	5	341	2·8 1·5
	6	355	2·3 1·2

Victoria

4 Plot the tidal stream at the start of the ground track.

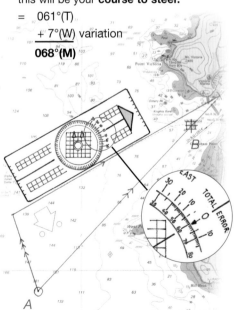

5 Measure the expected boat speed for one hour (9kn) and arc dividers from end of tidal stream to cross the ground track, this usually goes beyond or falls short of B.

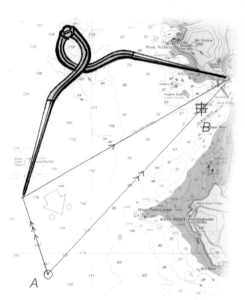

6 Measure direction of water track - this will be your **course to steer.**

$$= \ 061°(T)$$
$$+ \ 7°(W) \ \text{variation}$$
$$\mathbf{068°(M)}$$

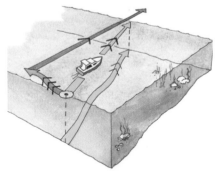

Although you are steering 068°(M) you are maintaining your shortest COG or ground track (051°M) A to B.

7 Consider leeway. Head up 5° or 10° into the wind if necessary.

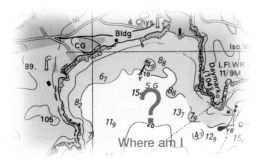

Where am I

A VISUAL FIX

Three point fix

Take bearings on charted objects to fix your position.

Draw the bearings on the chart.

Bearings rarely line up as a perfect fix.

If bearings are too close together - error is greater.

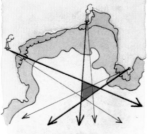

Your position will be where the lines intersect. Use closer objects for greater accuracy.

Error produces a cocked hat.

Don't use objects that will give a poor angle of cut.

Transit and bearing

Line up two charted objects to make a transit - this gives you a very accurate position line. Obtain a fix by taking a bearing on another object, preferably at about 90° to the transit.

chimney and flag staff

The simplest fix

Plot your position as you pass a charted object.

Bearing and contour

Fix your position by taking a bearing on a charted object as you cross a contour – don't forget to allow for the height of tide.

070°(T)

A GPS FIX

A GPS receiver obtains a fix from signals transmitted by orbiting satellites - this gives a position which is accurate to about 15 metres.

The simplest way to use GPS is to plot your position from the Latitude and Longitude given on the display.

36°25'30 S
114°57'30 E

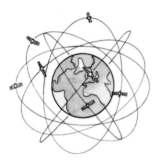

It can also give:

* your current course and speed over the ground

* information about your position in relation to waypoints (see next page).

GPS is generally reliable and accurate but, as with all electronics, it can go wrong. The main things that can affect it are:

* power or aerial failure
* transmissions from mobile phones
* interruption or changes to the satellite system.

Yeoman Plotter

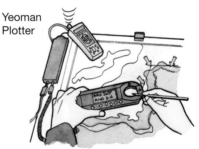

This type of plotter provides a link between the chart and the GPS.

Always back up your GPS position with information from another source such as:

IALA B buoyage

A charted object.

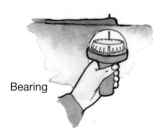

Bearing

Depth allowing for tide.

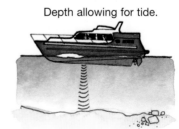

Keep a record of your position at regular intervals on the chart and in the ship's log.

50°11'20N
004°40'30W

Waypoints (WPTs) are tools to help you navigate. They are positions stored in the memory of a GPS and used as reference points.

For example you could use a WPT placed at the entrance of a harbour to help guide you safely into port or as part of a route.

You obtain WPTs from:

- the chart – select the position and measure the lat. and long.
- publications such as almanacs, directories and magazines - check before use.

The GPS display can show the direction and distance to a WPT and your COG and SOG.

Be careful when you input a WPT into a GPS.

Always check that the direction and distance given by the GPS matches that measured on the chart. Any difference means you have probably input the WPT lat and long incorrectly.

Never input a WPT straight from a book or magazine.

Always plot it on a chart to check your route.

Plot your WPT adjacent to rather than directly on charted objects - you could hit them.

In busy areas bear in mind that lots of boats could be using the same WPT.

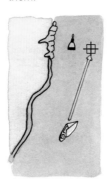

OTHER WAYS OF USING WAYPOINTS

You can plot your position quickly and simply by entering easily found positions as WPTs.

The GPS will give you a direction and distance to the WPT and you can plot these to give a fix.

This is easier, quicker and less prone to error than plotting lat. and long. but double check that you have entered the WPT correctly.

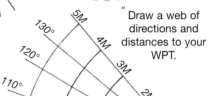

46°07'.20N
006°15'.00W

You can also use the WPT that you are travelling to.

Plotting at speed

Conventional plotting can be difficult on a fast boat at speed.

Navigation must be pre-planned.

Draw a web of directions and distances to your WPT.

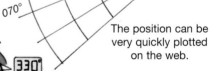

130°
120°
110°
100°
90°
080°
070°

5M 4M 3M 2M 1M

102°
3.3M

The position can be very quickly plotted on the web.

Be careful

Remember – GPS doesn't allow for tidal stream.

shortest route

intended track

longer route

[330°]

[031°]

[050°]

Always pre-plan a course to steer to allow for tidal stream – it's more efficient.

It seems easy to just steer the direction that the GPS gives to a WPT but if there is significant cross tide you:

• will sail a longer route

• could put the boat in danger.

Two buoyage systems exist in the world, IALA A and IALA B. The difference affects the colour and light characteristics of lateral marks.

IALA A is used in Europe, Africa, Russia, India, Australia and New Zealand.

IALA B, which is illustrated on page 64, is used in the USA, South America, the parts of the Caribbean, South East Asia and Canada.

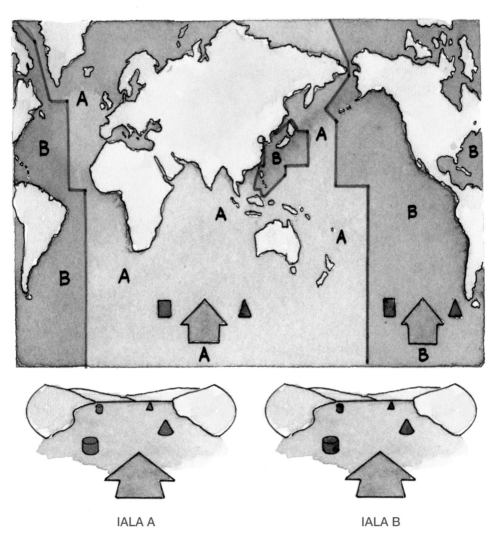

IALA A   IALA B

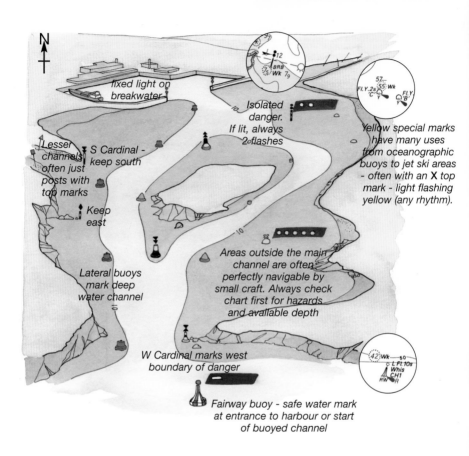

N

fixed light on breakwater

Isolated danger. If lit, always 2 flashes

Yellow special marks have many uses from oceanographic buoys to jet ski areas - often with an **X** top mark - light flashing yellow (any rhythm).

Lesser channels often just posts with top marks

S Cardinal - keep south

Keep east

Lateral buoys mark deep water channel

Areas outside the main channel are often perfectly navigable by small craft. Always check chart first for hazards and available depth

W Cardinal marks west boundary of danger

Fairway buoy - safe water mark at entrance to harbour or start of buoyed channel

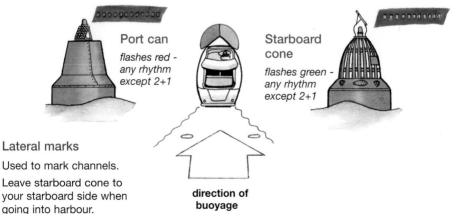

Port can

flashes red - any rhythm except 2+1

Starboard cone

flashes green - any rhythm except 2+1

Lateral marks

Used to mark channels.

Leave starboard cone to your starboard side when going into harbour.

direction of buoyage

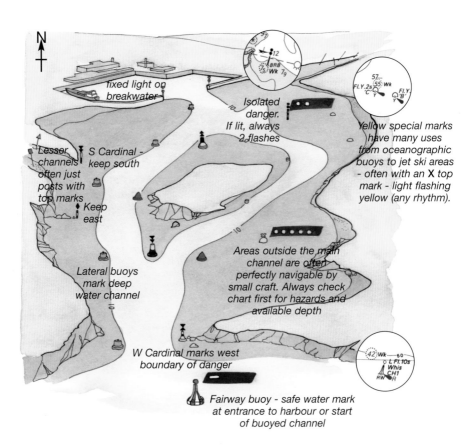

N

fixed light on breakwater

Isolated danger.
If lit, always 2 flashes

Yellow special marks have many uses from oceanographic buoys to jet ski areas – often with an X top mark – light flashing yellow (any rhythm).

Lesser channels often just posts with top marks

S Cardinal - keep south

Keep east

Lateral buoys mark deep water channel

Areas outside the main channel are often perfectly navigable by small craft. Always check chart first for hazards and available depth

W Cardinal marks west boundary of danger

Fairway buoy - safe water mark at entrance to harbour or start of buoyed channel

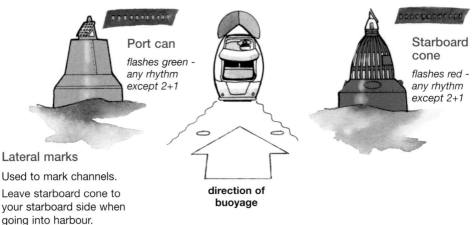

Port can

flashes green - any rhythm except 2+1

Starboard cone

flashes red - any rhythm except 2+1

direction of buoyage

Lateral marks

Used to mark channels.

Leave starboard cone to your starboard side when going into harbour.

Cardinals

Cardinal marks warn of danger and remain constant thoughout the IALA system.

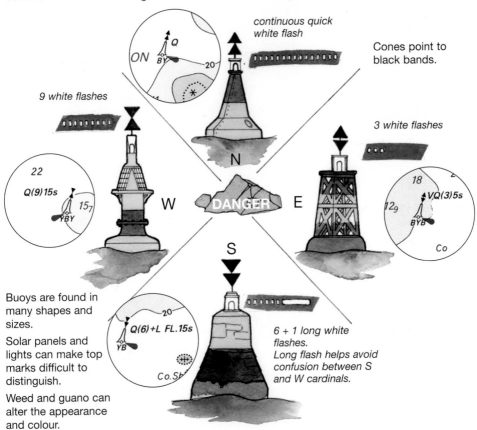

continuous quick white flash

Cones point to black bands.

9 white flashes

3 white flashes

N

W

DANGER

E

S

Buoys are found in many shapes and sizes.

Solar panels and lights can make top marks difficult to distinguish.

Weed and guano can alter the appearance and colour.

6 + 1 long white flashes. Long flash helps avoid confusion between S and W cardinals.

Emergency wreck-marking buoy

Light - Alternating blue and yellow, 1 second flashes with an interval of 0.5 second.

Emergency wreck-marking buoy, placed at the site of a new wreck. Remains in place until the wreck has been dealt with.

Preferred channel marks IALA A

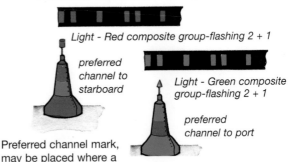

Light - Red composite group-flashing 2 + 1

preferred channel to starboard

Light - Green composite group-flashing 2 + 1

preferred channel to port

Preferred channel mark, may be placed where a channel splits in two, indicating the preferred channel.

SECTOR LIGHTS

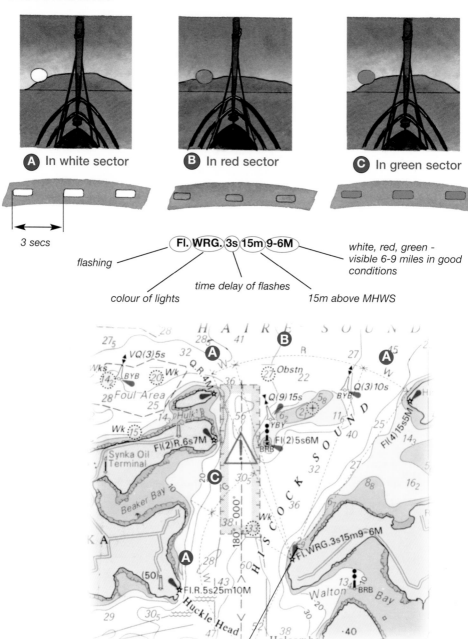

A In white sector

B In red sector

C In green sector

3 secs

flashing — FL. WRG. 3s 15m 9-6M — *white, red, green - visible 6-9 miles in good conditions*

colour of lights

time delay of flashes

15m above MHWS

e.g. Evans Head Light House

LEADING LIGHTS guide you in and out of harbour. eg. Setter Hall Marina, Dunbarton.

| Too far to starboard | On course | Too far to port |

LIGHTHOUSE e.g. Leslie Head Lighthouse, on Synka Island.

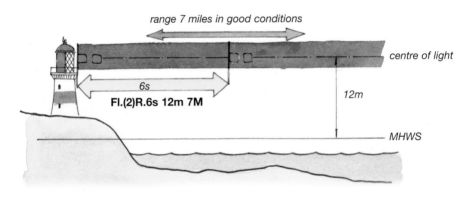

range 7 miles in good conditions

centre of light

6s

Fl.(2)R.6s 12m 7M

12m

MHWS

Other light characteristics

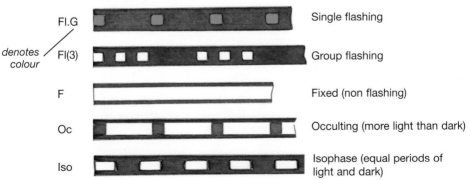

Fl.G		Single flashing
denotes colour Fl(3)		Group flashing
F		Fixed (non flashing)
Oc		Occulting (more light than dark)
Iso		Isophase (equal periods of light and dark)

Pilotage is the art of inshore navigation when you have visual references to help you find your way along the coast and in and out of harbour.

There may be lots of different hazards so good planning is essential.

Don't spend too much time down below – you will soon lose track of where you are and put yourself in danger.

Making a good plan means you can navigate from on deck.

THINGS YOU MIGHT NEED TO PLAN FOR

Rocks

Shoals & shallows

Shipping channels

How an expanse of water changes...

at high water   and low water

Chain ferries

Harbour byelaws

e.g. Small craft channels

SPEED LIMIT
(5)
IN HARBOUR

Speed restriction in channel

Effect of tide

A different port may have a change of buoyage system – here it is IALA A buoyage

Transits

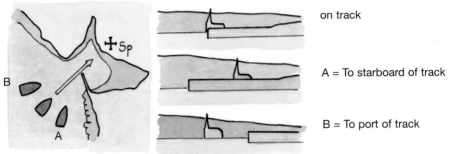

on track

A = To starboard of track

B = To port of track

Contours

You can work out where you are when you cross a contour and they can be followed in poor visibility.

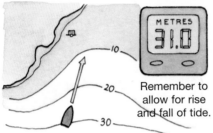

Remember to allow for rise and fall of tide.

Clearing bearing

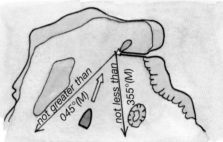

You can go anywhere between the two bearings.

Back bearing

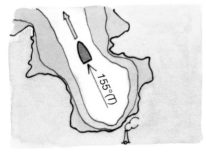

Bearing + distance

IALA B buoyage

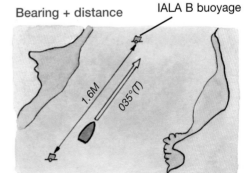

Work this out in advance so you know when and where to expect the next buoy

Turning points

Turn when chimney bears 320°(T)

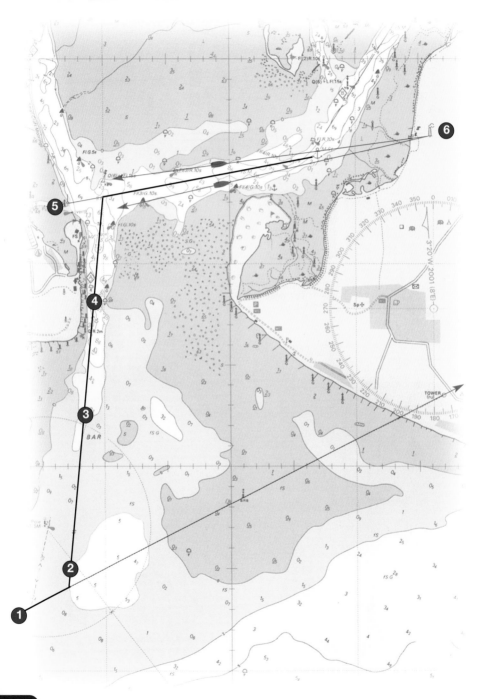

1 Transit

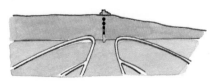

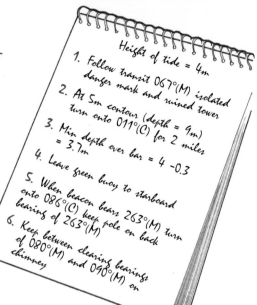

Height of tide = 4m

1. Follow transit 067°(M) isolated danger mark and ruined tower

2. At 5m contour (depth = 9m) turn onto 011°(C) for 2 miles

3. Min depth over bar = 4 -0.3 = 3.7m

4. Leave green buoy to starboard

5. When beacon bears 263°(M) turn onto 086°(C) keep pole on back bearing of 263°(M)

6. Keep between clearing bearings of 080°(M) and 090°(M) on chimney

2 Contour

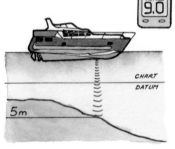

CHART
DATUM

5m

3 Clearance over bar

4 Positive identification of marks
IALA A buoyage

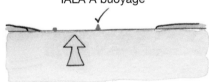

5 Back bearing

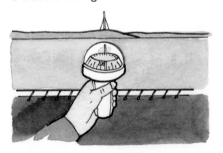

6 Clearing lines

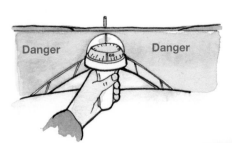

Danger   Danger

General overview

Low and high-pressure systems dictate our weather. They revolve in different directions, depending on which hemisphere they inhabit. Where you are cruising on the earth's surface will dictate whether lows, highs or a mixture of both dictate your weather. In the UK, low-pressure systems dictate our weather. In many places in the Southern hemisphere cold fronts dictate the weather scene.

In the Northern Hemisphere Low pressure systems revolve anticlockwise and Highs revolve clockwise

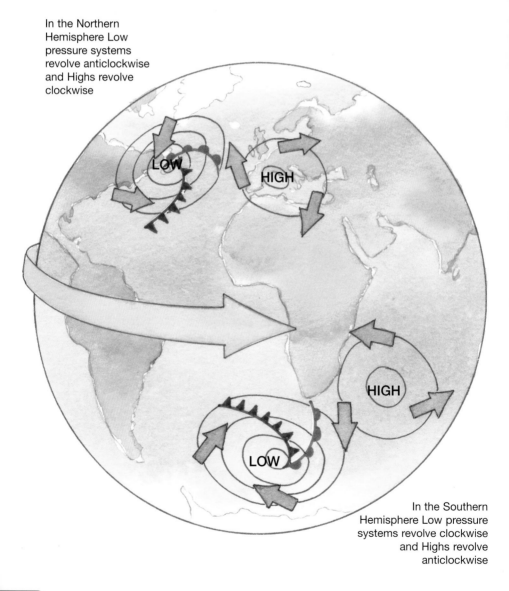

In the Southern Hemisphere Low pressure systems revolve clockwise and Highs revolve anticlockwise

NORTHERN HEMISPHERE

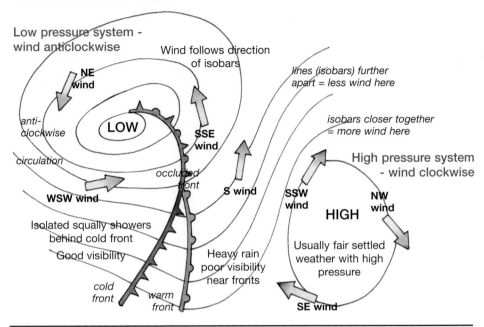

Low pressure system -
wind anticlockwise

Wind follows direction
of isobars

NE wind

lines (isobars) further
apart = less wind here

anti-clockwise

LOW

SSE wind

isobars closer together
= more wind here

circulation

High pressure system
- wind clockwise

occluded front

S wind

SSW wind

NW wind

WSW wind

HIGH

Isolated squally showers
behind cold front

Good visibility

Heavy rain
poor visibility
near fronts

Usually fair settled
weather with high
pressure

cold front

warm front

SE wind

SOUTHERN HEMISPHERE

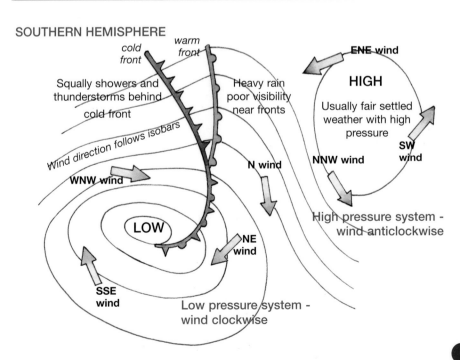

cold front

warm front

Squally showers and
thunderstorms behind
cold front

Heavy rain
poor visibility
near fronts

ENE wind

HIGH

Usually fair settled
weather with high
pressure

Wind direction follows isobars

WNW wind

N wind

NNW wind

SW wind

High pressure system -
wind anticlockwise

LOW

NE wind

SSE wind

Low pressure system -
wind clockwise

Shipping Forecast Areas

Get to know your local Forecast Areas

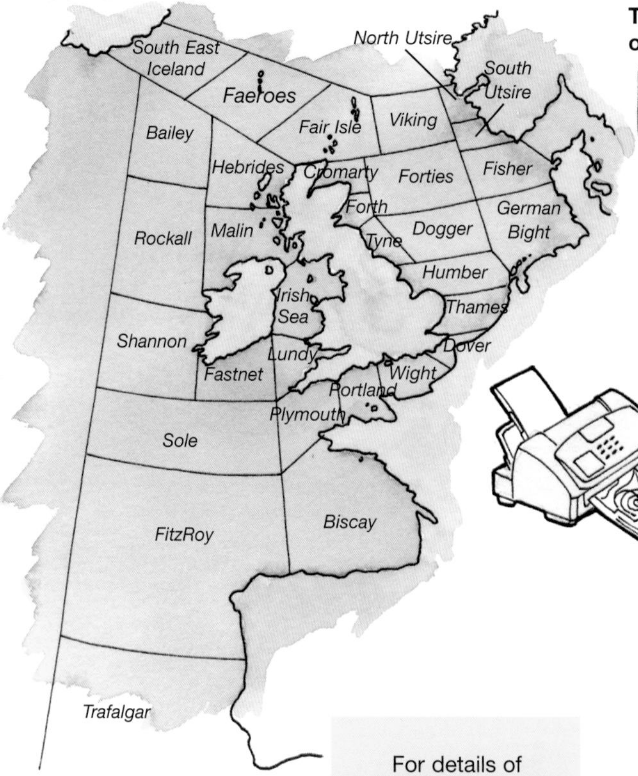
South East Iceland
North Utsire
South Utsire
Faeroes
Bailey
Fair Isle
Viking
Hebrides
Cromarty
Forties
Fisher
Forth
German Bight
Rockall
Malin
Tyne
Dogger
Humber
Irish Sea
Thames
Shannon
Lundy
Dover
Fastnet
Wight
Portland
Plymouth
Sole
Biscay
FitzRoy
Trafalgar

There are many different ways to obtain a forecast.

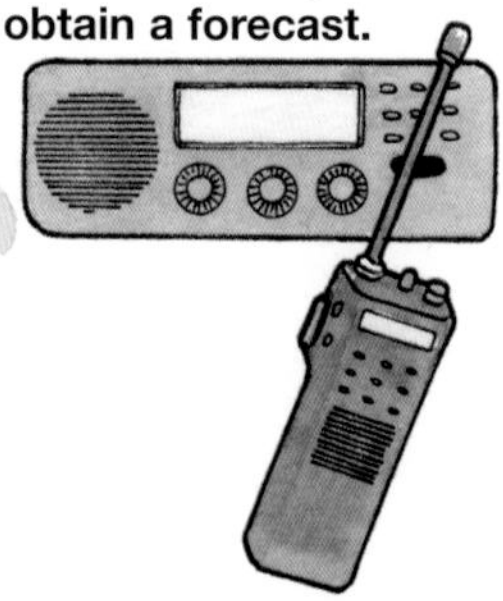

Marine safety information broadcasts on VHF by Coastguard.

Metfax

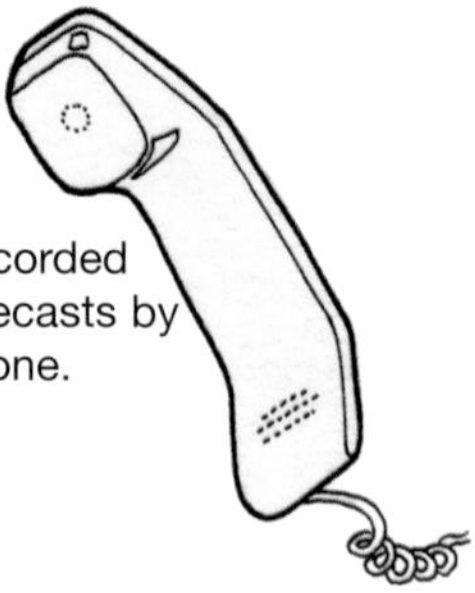

Recorded forecasts by phone.

For details of forecast times etc. look in an almanac or RYA book of Weather Forecasts (G5)

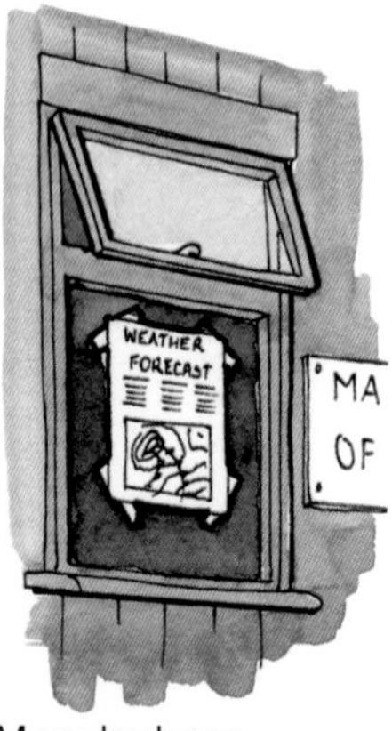
WEATHER FORECAST
MA
OF

Many harbour and marina offices post a forecast.

Internet

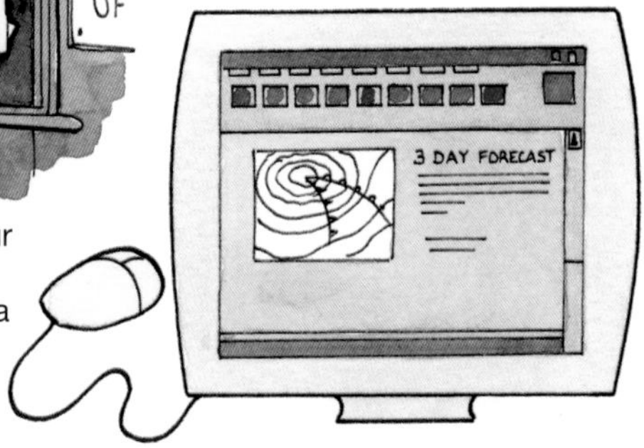
3 DAY FORECAST

Teletext

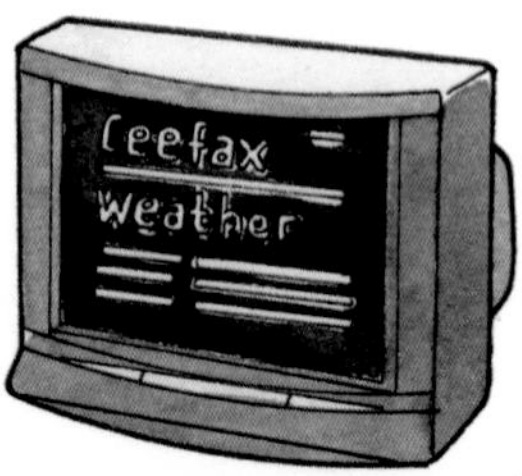
Ceefax
weather

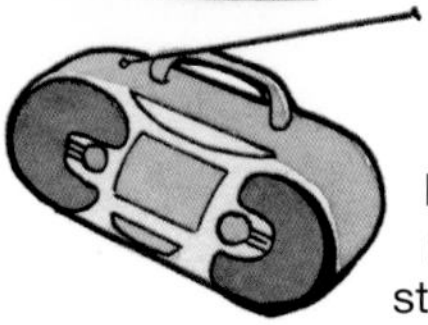

Local radio stations.

TERMS USED IN FORECASTS

Gale warnings	If average wind is expected to be F8 or more, or gusts 43-51kn.
Strong wind warnings	If average wind is expected to be F6 or F7. F6 is often called a 'yachtsman's gale'.
Imminent	Within 6 hrs of time of issue of warning.
Soon	Within 6-12 hrs of time of issue of warning.
Later	More than 12 hrs from time of issue of warning.
Visibility	*Good* - greater than 5 miles *Moderate* - between 2 - 5 miles. *Poor* - 1,000m to 2 miles. Fog less than 1,000m.
Fair	No significant precipitation.
Backing	Wind changing in an anticlockwise direction eg NW to SW.
Veering	Wind changing in a clockwise direction eg NE to SE.
General synopsis	How and where the weather systems are moving.
Sea states	*Smooth* - wave height 0.2 - 0.5m *Slight* - wave height 0.5 - 1.25m. *Moderate* - wave height 1.25 - 2.5m *Rough* - wave height 2.5 - 4m. *Very rough* - wave height 4 - 6m.

LAND AND SEA BREEZES

Land breeze

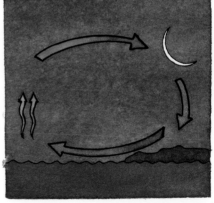

Sea breeze

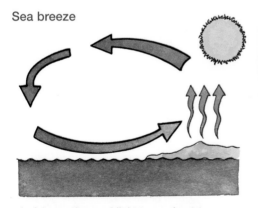

In fair weather and light to moderate offshore wind, a sea breeze is likely to develop. Warm air rises over land, it then cools, descends and blows onshore. Wind up to force 4 in strength.

This occurs on a clear night when the air cools over land and flows downhill and out to sea, particularly from river estuaries.

Wind usually no more than force 2- 3 except near mountains.

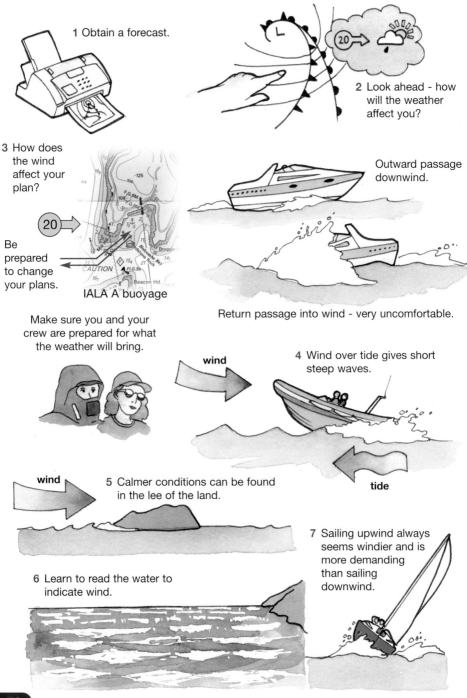

1 Obtain a forecast.

2 Look ahead - how will the weather affect you?

3 How does the wind affect your plan?

Be prepared to change your plans.

IALA A buoyage

Outward passage downwind.

Return passage into wind - very uncomfortable.

Make sure you and your crew are prepared for what the weather will bring.

wind

4 Wind over tide gives short steep waves.

tide

wind

5 Calmer conditions can be found in the lee of the land.

6 Learn to read the water to indicate wind.

7 Sailing upwind always seems windier and is more demanding than sailing downwind.

1 Light airs 1 - 3 knots
Ripples.
Sail - drifting conditions
Power - fast planing conditions

2 Light breeze 4 - 6 knots
Small wavelets.
Sail - full mainsail and large genoa
Power - fast planing conditions

3 Gentle breeze 7 - 10 knots
Occasional crests.
Sail - full sail
Power - fast planing conditions

4 Moderate 11 - 16 knots
Frequent white horses.
Sail - reduce headsail size
Power - may have to slow down if wind
against tide

5 Fresh breeze 17 - 21 knots
Moderate waves, many white crests.
Sail - reef mainsail
Power - reduce speed to prevent
slamming when going upwind

6 Strong breeze 22 - 27 knots
Large waves, white foam crests.
Sail - reef main and reduce headsail
Power - displacement speed

7 Near gale 28 - 33 knots
Sea heaps up, spray, breaking waves,
foam blows in streaks.
Sail - deep reefed main, small jib
Power - displacement speed

8 Gale 34 - 40 knots
Moderately high waves, breaking crests.
Sail - deep reefed main, storm jib
Power - displacement speed, stem waves

9 Severe gale 41 - 47 knots
High waves, spray affects visibility.
Sail - trysail and storm jib
Power - displacement speed, stem waves

10 Storm 48 - 55 knots
Very high waves, long breaking crests.
Survival conditions

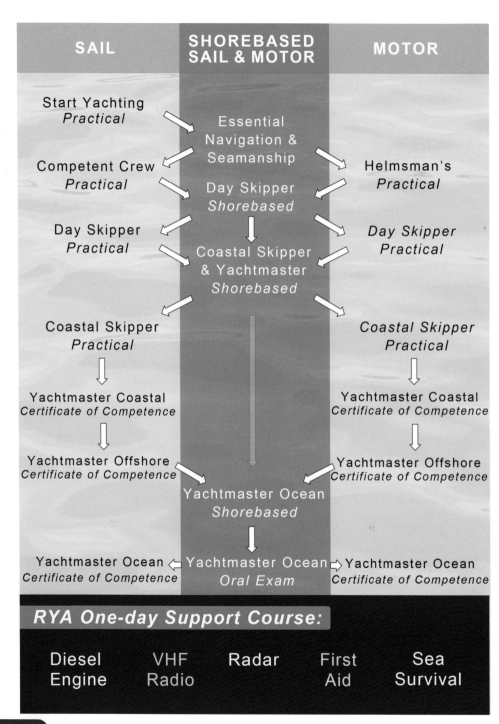

SAIL	SHOREBASED SAIL & MOTOR	MOTOR
Start Yachting *Practical*	Essential Navigation & Seamanship	
Competent Crew *Practical*	Day Skipper *Shorebased*	Helmsman's *Practical*
Day Skipper *Practical*	Coastal Skipper & Yachtmaster *Shorebased*	Day Skipper *Practical*
Coastal Skipper *Practical*		Coastal Skipper *Practical*
Yachtmaster Coastal *Certificate of Competence*		Yachtmaster Coastal *Certificate of Competence*
Yachtmaster Offshore *Certificate of Competence*	Yachtmaster Ocean *Shorebased*	Yachtmaster Offshore *Certificate of Competence*
Yachtmaster Ocean *Certificate of Competence*	Yachtmaster Ocean *Oral Exam*	Yachtmaster Ocean *Certificate of Competence*

RYA One-day Support Course:

Diesel Engine	VHF Radio	Radar	First Aid	Sea Survival

RYA MEMBERSHIP APPLICATION

IT'S ALL ABOUT YOU AND THE BOATING YOU DO

Be part of it

One of boating's biggest attractions is its freedom from rules and regulations. As an RYA member you'll play an active part in keeping it that way, as well as benefiting from free expert advice and information, plus discounts on a wide range of boating products, charts and publications.

To join the RYA, please complete the application form below and send it to The Membership Department, RYA, RYA House, Ensign Way, Hamble, Southampton, Hampshire SO31 4YA. You can also join online at www.rya.org.uk, or by phoning the membership department on +44 (0) 23 8060 4159. Whichever way you choose to apply, you can save money by paying by Direct Debit. A Direct Debit instruction is on the back of this form.

	Title	Forename	Surname	Gender	Date of Birth
Applicant ❶				M/F	D D / M M / Y Y Y Y
Applicant ❷				M/F	D D / M M / Y Y Y Y
Applicant ❸				M/F	D D / M M / Y Y Y Y
Applicant ❹				M/F	D D / M M / Y Y Y Y

Address

Post Code

E-mail Applicant ❶

E-mail Applicant ❷

E-mail Applicant ❸

E-mail Applicant ❹

Home Tel

Day Time Tel

Mobile Tel

Type of membership required (Tick Box) – Annual Rate

Junior (0-11)	£5 by direct debit	£5 non direct debit rate
Youth (12-17)	£10 by direct debit	£15 non direct debit rate
Under 25	£20 by direct debit	£25 non direct debit rate
Personal	£40 by direct debit	£45 non direct debit rate
Family*	£60 by direct debit	£65 non direct debit rate

Save money by completing the Direct Debit form overleaf

Please number up to three boating interests in order, with number one being your principal interest

- Yacht Racing
- Personal Watercraft
- Powerboat Racing
- Yacht Cruising
- Sportboats & RIBs
- Canal Cruising
- Dinghy Racing
- Windsurfing
- River Cruising
- Dinghy Cruising
- Motor Boating

* *Family Membership: 2 adults plus any under 18s all living at the same address. Prices valid until 30/9/2013. One discount voucher is accepted for individual memberships, and two discount vouchers are accepted for family membership.*

IMPORTANT In order to provide you with membership benefits the details provided by you on this form and in the course of your membership will be maintained on a database. If you do not wish to receive information on member services and benefits please tick here ☐ . By applying for membership of the RYA you agree to be bound by the RYA's standard terms and conditions (copies on request or at www.rya.org.uk)

Signature

Date D D / M M / Y Y Y Y

Source Code 0 7 7

Joining Point Code

GET MORE FROM
YOUR
BOATING
SUPPORT THE
RYA

RYA
Be part of it

PAY BY DIRECT DEBIT – AND SAVE MONEY

Instructions to your Bank or Building Society to pay by Direct Debit

Please fill in the form and send to:
Membership Department, Royal Yachting Association, RYA House, Ensign Way, Hamble,
Southampton, Hampshire SO31 4YA.

Name and full postal address of your Bank/Building Society

To the Manager _____ Bank/Building Society

Address

Postcode

Name(s) of Account Holder(s)

Branch Sort Code

☐☐ – ☐☐ – ☐☐

Bank/Building Society Account Number

☐☐☐☐☐☐☐☐

Originator's Identification Number

| 9 | 5 | 5 | 2 | 1 | 3 |

RYA Membership Number (For office use only)

Instructions to your Bank or Building Society

Please pay Royal Yachting Association Direct Debits from the account detailed in this instruction subject to the safeguards assured by The Direct Debit Guarantee. I understand that this instruction may remain with the Royal Yachting Association and, if so, details will be passed electronically to my Bank/Building Society.

Signature(s)

Date: D D / M M / Y Y Y Y